WHAT'S AGE GOT
TO DO WITH IT?

Ralph Merten, 88

WHAT'S AGE GOT TO DO WITH IT?

Kelly Ferrin

ALTI PUBLISHING

Consult your physician before beginning any fitness program. The contents presented herein are not intended as therapy, recommendations, or as substitutes for treatment by a physician or other health-care professional. The accounts described in this book are only the personal experiences of those listed.

Ferrin, Kelly, 1960–
    What's age got to do with it? / Kelly Ferrin.
        p. cm.
    ISBN 1-883051-21-5
    1. Aged—United States —Biography.   I. Title.
HQ1064.U5F443   1998   98-24206
305.26'092'273—dc21   CIP

ALTI Publishing
P.O. Box 28025, San Diego, California 92198-0025, USA
Telephone: (619) 485-1616
E-mail: whilbig@altipublishing.com

Copyediting: Sherri Schottlaender
Cover design: Foster & Foster
Interior design: Kathleen Thorne-Thomsen
Photograph on page 49, courtesy *Detroit Free Press*
                on page 100, courtesy Los Angeles Lakers
                on page 189, courtesy Cooper Fitness Center
                on page 193, courtesy Schwinn Cycling & Fitness, Inc.

Printed in the United States of America
10 9 8 7 6 5 4 3 2 1

ISBN 1-883051-21-5
Distributed to the trade by National Book Network (800) 462-6420

Ten Secrets to Ageless Living

🕊 Never let age get in the way of life.

🕊 Stay curious, explore, discover, and continue to learn new things.

🕊 Play, have fun, be happy, and maintain a zest for life by being vital.

🕊 Keep the brain and the body busy; stimulate the mind, eat healthy, exercise.

🕊 Smile, laugh, maintain a sense of humor, and always stay young at heart.

🕊 Have a positive attitude, outlook, and be optimistic to overcome challenges.

🕊 Believe in yourself by having faith, hope, spirit, value, meaning, and purpose.

🕊 Stay connected, engaged, creative, and useful by continuing to contribute.

🕊 Find fulfillment, peace, serenity, and self-esteem by giving back—volunteer.

🕊 Enjoy and cherish healthy relationships with loved ones, friends, and family.

🕊 The Ageless Golden Rule 🕊

Live long, live well, laugh often, love much . . .
and always enjoy life's journey.

Dedication

To all those who believe age is just a number

and whose lives have inspired me

to share the secrets of what's possible with age.

Acknowledgements

There are many who deserve thanks for making this project possible, including supportive family, friends, and all those who shared their stories. Special thanks to ALTI Publishing, and in particular, Wayne Hilbig and Sandra O'Rourke, for their dedicated effort, support, guidance, and genuine commitment to books like these . . . in an effort to make the world a better and happier place for us all.

My most sincere professional gratitude goes to Ken Dychtwald, Ph.D., CEO and author of *Age Wave,* for his incredible insight and vision on aging. Also thanks to the numerous other inspirational mentors including James E. Birren, Ph.D., Dr. Walter M. Bortz, II, Dr. Robert N. Butler, Etta Clark, William Evans, Ph.D., Betty Friedan, Connie Goldman, Jack LaLanne, Gail Sheehy, and Dr. Andrew Weil who have also enlightened me and contributed greatly to my passion for this field.

And most of all I want to thank my buddy-lover, my husband, Tim, who has always believed in me and provided the love, magic, and never ending support that made this all happen.

Contents

Contents

Contents ❧

ꜱ Contents

How old
would "old" be
if we didn't know
how old "old" was?

If we really believed age was just a number, think how differently we would live our lives. Who says you can't hang glide at 90, run hurdles at 80, become an entrepreneur at 70, a full-time volunteer or adventurer at 60? What is "normal" for today's 70-, 80-, 90-, and 100-year-olds? It's not about rocking chairs anymore—more like rock climbing! Exploring, adventuring, volunteering, having a sense of meaning, purpose and a zest for life are ageless qualities that can be obtained at any age.

A definite trend is occurring—aging is changing. People are living longer, healthier lives than ever before and this extraordinary phenomenon is forever changing both the way we look at aging and the way we ourselves age. A new style is emerging as people determine what's really possible in their later years. The life cycle has changed and so have the rules—the majority of older adults today are healthy and happy and believe that these are among the best years of their lives. They're not concerned with avoiding aging—they've discovered the secrets by being and doing and are not letting age get in the way of living.

People are doing some extraordinary things as a result of living longer. In fact, so many are living their lives this way the question now becomes: Are these people really extraordinary . . . or has this become ordinary? Research validates what's occurring in today's new older adult population. Scientific breakthroughs in healthcare and medical technology have enabled us to live longer, while studies now also conclude that we do play a significant role in determining both how long and how well we live.

It's about choices, beliefs, and attitudes and the influence they have on behaviors that affect our health and longevity. With aging being redefined, it's time we update our beliefs about what our later years can be, because what we believe profoundly affects our actions, and therefore, our lives.

There are a variety of ways to age—it's no longer a time of inevitable decline. Yet because we've never been a society with millions of healthy older adults serving as role models as they do today, perhaps we age because we expect to age and have been conditioned to believe age is a time of decline, because that's all we've ever known or believed was possible. If the majority of aging studies have been done on the sick and frail in nursing homes, it's not surprising that our image of aging is negative. But are those the only seniors there are? Of course not, yet because they were the ones studied, they became our image of aging. The positive aging images have been far and few between . . . until now.

I always believed there was another side of aging because I'd seen healthy, active, vital, and productive seniors who were the same age as those studied in institutions, but who were living very differently. Clearly, it wasn't just chronological age—other contributing factors affected how people lived well in their later years and prevented the decline so many believed was automatic with age.

My grandparents were, and still remain today, my most cherished role models of aging well. In his eighties, my grandfather, Dede, did chin-ups at our family picnics—smiling and flexing his incredibly developed biceps. My grandmother, Nana, is still healthy, sharp as a tack, and very independent at 92. My parents, both in their seventies, are also very active—working, volunteering, playing golf, traveling, socializing—just loving life! Many others who I don't even know also confirmed my belief that there was more to aging than just a number.

Current statistics show that 95.8 percent of Americans age 65 to 74, live independently. At the introduction of Social Security in 1935, only 4 percent survived past 65. In the past fifteen years there's been a 15 percent decline in disabilities among people over 80, and the fastest growing segment of our U.S. population is the 85-plus age group. These are the facts, and they represent a considerably different image of aging than what most people think.

According to John W. Rowe, M.D., director of a long-range study on successful aging, we now control much of our own aging process: 30 percent of the characteristics of aging are based on genetics, 70 percent are based on lifestyle. The choices we make on a daily basis have a direct effect on how we age.

Ken Dychtwald, Ph.D., co-author of *Age Wave* and a leading expert on aging issues, says that what many call aging is really a lifestyle issue. Studies show that 80 percent of the health problems of older adults are lifestyle-related, meaning that lifestyle can prevent, postpone the onset, and slow down the pain or debilitation of many of the conditions we automatically blame on age.

This is exciting news, because it's never too late to in-corporate healthy behaviors into our lifestyles and bene-fit from them. And since we're more susceptible to problems as we grow older, now we know that practic-ing good health habits can make a difference in our quality of life.

A new mindset may be needed first, because what we think is possible in our later years will directly affect the choices we make, and thus our aging process. If we be-lieve that our later years can be a time of good health and vitality, then we're more likely to practice the be-haviors necessary to ensure this reality.

There is no magic formula to guarantee a long life filled with good health and happiness, but there are a variety of secrets that together can definitely increase our odds of getting older without getting old. Many in their later years are doing things people half their age can't do, and there are reasons why they can . . . and why others can, too.

This book takes a refreshing look at what's right with age. No pills or potions, just true life stories of extraordi-nary aging which offer hope, insight, and inspiration for what's possible with age by learning what's worked for others. There's definitely a right way to do it, and this book shares the secrets of those who have.

These stories feature humble people. They don't want to brag or boast, nor do they think that what they are doing is extraordinary. They do what they do because they enjoy it, and it makes them feel good mentally, physically, and soulfully. If their stories and experiences can help change beliefs and mindsets about what's pos-sible with age or encourage and motivate others to feel good, too, then perhaps this book will serve as a valuable tool to create a new style of positive, healthy aging for years to come and forever change the way we age.

It's time to share the secrets of aging well, related by those who are actually doing it. Call them secrets, or perhaps choices these people made in order to age well: There are definite similarities, but each individual also has a personal story that makes their journey unique. By experiencing the adventures taken by others, perhaps this book will inspire an adventure in you and forever change the way you age, too!

There is no specific order to the book . . . open it up to any page, at any time, and you will be inspired. The only rule is: Never let age get in the way of life!

Kelly Ferrin

On the journey of life, the road offers different paths . . . the choices we make often determine our direction and destination. Yet we all desire to travel the path of good health and happiness with a zest for life and a feeling of fulfillment each new day, regardless of our age.

This book provides a road map for an adventure; it reveals how others have found this destination, a place where age is just a number and few feel their actual age. It is a place where age and life are celebrated, instilling a feeling of hope about what's possible. It's an attainable destination . . . the destination is within ourselves.

The secrets of aging well lie within these pages: words of wisdom gained from experience, which are applicable and enlightening to us all. Enchanting, engaging, inspiring, and fun . . . they teach us to always enjoy life's journey!

Love, health, and happiness always,

The Age Angel

Ethel Asfahl, 93

Enid, Oklahoma

E thel took "early retirement" at the age of 82 from the company she and her husband started forty-six years earlier—one she ran alone, for twenty-three of those years, after his sudden death. She lives her life around one simple motto: "I believe anyone can do anything they set their mind to. Anything is possible and you can be anything you want to be . . . but you have to believe in yourself enough to make it happen!"

It's a wisdom that often only comes with age, and one many young people in Ethel's area, from middle teens to young adults, are coming to hear. Each week anywhere from seven to thirty visitors stop by Ethel's home for a cup of companionship . . . with maybe a teaspoon of wisdom sprinkled in, too. Her ten grandchildren and four great-grandchildren also love their special "alone" time with her—to talk and share their thoughts, so it's no wonder Ethel chose to take early retirement!

The fact that Ethel persevered on her own and didn't let anything stop her may be part of what draws the youth to her today. She is a pillar of positive thinking encouraging others to never stop trying nor accept their limitations. She instills in them the importance of attitude and a belief that things will always get better, saying a cheery disposition is part of her genetic makeup.

"Some people think getting older is about uselessness and institutions . . . but not for me. Wisdom comes with getting older, and I enjoy helping others. Good genes support my positive attitude—I've always had excellent health. I read without glasses, have all my original teeth, am never sick, don't take any vitamins or medicines, exercise only when I do my house- or yardwork, and eat what I want and when my body says it's hungry. Basically, I do exactly as I please and think that's the way to live," Ethel said. "Scientists feed us all these facts and figures, tell us to do one thing—then the next day it's something different—forget it! I say you don't have to do what everyone else does . . . do what's best for you!"

Her advice for living a long life is: don't fight it—it can be the very best time of your life. She doesn't understand why people are so caught up in doing everything they can just to try to stay young, especially when later life has so much more to offer.

Having a strong foundation is also essential, and Ethel recognizes that her faith, hard work, discipline, and taking care of her health have contributed greatly to how she feels today. She continues to share this wisdom with the youth and tells them there is much more to life than fancy automobiles, beautiful homes, and things money can buy.

"It's all about spirituality and faith, which becomes a way of life—and having a healthy attitude and outlook on life starts with this faith. But it's not a faith that has to be preached . . . it's a way of life. Walk the talk and live it! It's just that simple."

And maybe that's why people listen.

Florence Askin, 98

Saskatchewan, Canada

You're never too old for a birthday party—with cake, ice cream, and yes, even candles! Florence believes birthdays are for celebrating life, so you can be assured that her party invitations will be in the mail for her 100th birthday bash—which may just be the best party yet!

Florence hasn't let age slow her down, in fact, it seems the only slow thing that's in her life is her 1967 Dodge, which tops out at 50 MPH. But that's O.K. with Florence; she still drives it anyway, but only in the summer and just around town because she's afraid she might hold up traffic if she drove it on the highway. "I use it on errands to the store and for visits with my friends—it gets me out and about and keeps me independent," Florence stated.

And independent she is—while some might think it's depressing being a widow and living alone, Florence has a good attitude and keeps herself busy. She says she has little to complain about and thinks this has been key to her longevity.

She also attributes her long and healthy life to "hard work" and says aging is no time to slack off and take it easy. "A group of us seniors drive to the next town to a motel pool and hot tub where we can do our water exercises," Florence said. "I've been doing this since I was 84, and of course, I am the oldest member."

Florence knows exercise is good for her, but she also believes being with her friends is good for her soul. On the days when she's not much in the mood to go, the thought of missing socializing with her friends inspires her to pull herself together and off she goes. Up until the age of 77, she played the sport of curling—a wonderful form of skilled exercise played on a sheet of ice—so in comparison, the pool workout is a piece of cake!

And Florence likes cake you know—especially birthday cake. She tries to keep things in balance, smile and laugh every day, and continues to live her life by looking for the good in things—which will always be her secret birthday wish!

Walt Bailey, 83

San Diego, California

H is wife jokingly refers to him as "the professional volunteer", and they laugh about the idea that he's missing a gene . . . the "say no" one, in particular. But these activities have made a difference in Walt's life, and in the lives of others, too.

"The choices we make determine our life," Walt said. "Being from a close-knit family, I grew up helping others so that foundation has stayed with me and influences the choices I make." Serving others is something Walt is very comfortable with; talking about it, he is not. But a volunteer he is, has been, and always will be.

"It started when my sons were in Boy Scouts. I was involved with them and actually stayed on for several years even after they left the program," Walt remembered. "I've been a volunteer for the search and rescue team for the last thirty years. And recently I've combined my love of kids and the rescue work by participating in a community education program called Hug a Tree. When children are lost, we teach them to stay where they are and to hug a tree—then we'll be able to come and find them!"

As one of the founders of his company's retiree club, Walt is active in the community with toy drives, a bike refurbishing program for children, and an airplane restoration program for exhibits at the Aerospace Museum. Helping others, having projects, and feeling useful have all played significant parts in Walt's healthy retirement. In some respects, volunteering has *become* his work, serving almost the same amount of time in retirement as he did working. Perhaps Walt is living the life he would have had if he'd chosen a different job path when he first started working.

"I've been a hospital emergency room volunteer for over twenty-five years, but recently I switched to the special-care nursery program. In some respect I've always had this suppressed desire to be a doctor. I spent a brief time serving as a first-aid emergency medical technician, but circumstances didn't allow me to be a physician. So it seems I've chosen to do my part in other ways. I've also been involved with the TLC program—Tender Loving Canines—bringing animals and hospital patients together, and I spent two years with the hospice division, too."

Of course, taking care of and serving others takes a lot of energy and requires one to be in relatively good health. Walt fortunately has both, but he believes that good health takes work. Like anything else in life, nothing worthwhile comes easy—it takes effort. "I'm a great believer in holistic medicine," Walt said. "I think there is a connection between what you think and how you feel—the mind over matter deal is real. You can think yourself sick as much as you can think yourself well, to an extent, of course. As people grow older, many seem to blame their problems on age instead of looking at themselves and the choices they make."

In regard to staying healthy, Walt continues to make good choices—he runs a mile every day and believes in the importance of staying fit by being active and having balance in your life. By having an interest in life and the world he lives in, every day Walt strives to make a difference and contribute in a way that will live on long after he is gone.

John "Doc" Ball, 91

Eureka, California

There's no real creativity behind his nickname. John used to be a dentist, and his surfing buddies always called him "Doc." The name stuck and has stayed with him ever since, as has his love for surfing, which he now does on land.

"I guess you'd call me a sidewalk surfer these days! But hey, I'm still out there doing my thing: it just so happens that now I skateboard instead of surf! The water's too cold since I moved up north, and wetsuits are such a pain—so I decided to do something that gives me the same thrill without all the hassle."

Doc started surfing long before wetsuits were ever around. He believes his access to saltwater may have contributed to his longevity and why he's still skateboarding at the age of 91.

"Whether it was the saltwater or just all that good exercise, surfing is good for the body and soul," Doc said. "You use every part of your body out there, the muscles, the heart—it's all working when you're surfing."

Although Doc doesn't surf on a regular basis anymore, he still gets out a few times a year. He's not taking off on any major waves, but he's on a board in the ocean—and that's good enough for him.

He claims he stays in shape and experiences a similar joy to surfing when skateboarding. It keeps his reflexes keen, and he thinks it's helped keep his bones strong, too. He recently took a nasty fall and didn't even break a bone. "I was walking along the jetty, somehow lost my footing, and found myself falling about six feet down to the ground," Doc said. "I think my reflexes from years of surfing and skateboarding helped me know how to fall, because I didn't even have to go to the doctor! That's pretty remarkable, at my age."

Evelynn, his wife of fifty-four years, would rather Doc do something other than skateboard—he says she's always worried he's going to fall. But he fell from walking, not skateboarding, so it may be tough to get him to stop his fun anytime soon. "A man's got to have some fun—I'm not dead yet and I need to stay in shape. Plus, I think it's good exercise. It helps my balance and footwork, and most importantly—I really like it!"

Although he doesn't give much thought to the aging process, Doc believes two reasons he's lived so long are his diet and his faith. He especially prides himself on his self-taught knowledge of vitamins, nutrition supplements, and antioxidants. "People need to read and learn as much as they can about these things," Doc said. "It's hard to convince people that there might be something natural out there that's actually better for them than pharmaceuticals. It's an individual choice, so I just do what works for me."

As far as retirement goes and whether he ever thought he'd live this long, he simply says he's letting nature take its course. The way he figures it, the Lord has taken care of most of it and surfing's taken care of the rest . . . so he just goes with the flow!

Ruth Barati, 81

Soquel, California

L ike the phoenix that rose from the ashes, Ruth's newfound spirit has surfaced from the darkness of tragedy and death. Much like a butterfly that sheds its cocoon and sets itself free, she is experiencing a renewed life, one that has been there all along but took a deep internal search to find.

Her late husband was—and will always be—her lover, friend, and soulmate. George was an acclaimed musician, composer, and symphony conductor known all over the world. Tragically, he was found with a severe head injury, on a sidewalk where he had taken a stroll while Ruth taught a yoga class. He lingered in a coma for ten days before he died at the age of 83.

"He was ripped from my life, senselessly—and it's very difficult to find closure with such tragic and sudden death," Ruth said. "But because of our closeness and the incredible sense of connection we shared . . . we were as one, and forever will be."

Ruth's life was forever changed. Part of her was gone; her world had been turned upside down and nothing in life would ever be the same. Many days she wondered what the use was of even going on.

Yet there was another significant part of Ruth's life which eventually did help her find peace: yoga. For forty years she had practiced this gentle art, including twenty-five years of teaching, but it was now associated in her mind with a very dark time. It had become the "double-edged sword."

"My awareness of this beyond-physical connection George and I shared became very apparent to me when I reflected back to that tragic night. I was teaching a yoga class and remember looking at the clock at 9 P.M., which we later found out was the approximate time of the incident. I fell and lost my balance as I moved into a position, which is extremely unusual as an instructor, considering how long I've been doing these movements.

"At first I was totally embarrassed, but as I scrambled to pick myself up and resume the position, an overwhelming feeling, a powerful sense of rage and anger shot through my body. It was very strange, an unexplainable feeling. I didn't really understand it until later, when I put all the pieces together—I was experiencing the violence along with him somehow, through our non-physical connection."

Since both were highly respected in their fields, it was not unusual for Ruth and George to support each other by attending the other's sessions. After he died, Ruth wondered if she could ever do yoga again. Firstly, the shock and guilt that his death happened when she was teaching had caused her to wonder if she could have prevented it. Secondly, the foundation postures she had taught for more than half her life were suddenly forgotten. Yoga just didn't matter.

As is common for many widows, or anyone who loses a loved one, Ruth felt empty—there was no meaning or reason for being. It was a familiar feeling, because just four short years before this tragedy Ruth and George had lost their oldest daughter to breast cancer. Looking back now, she wonders if she ever healed from that, because the combination of the two was incomprehensible—the emotions were overwhelming.

"The lesson I had to learn was that I needed the complete inner life of yoga to help me heal my grief, the meditative and mental side that would help guide and connect me to a calm center from which I could summon at will serenity and peace."

Ruth always knew that yoga was more than physical, and she was now connecting within the spiritual aspect. Through this awareness, Ruth slowly began to heal and feel again. She describes it as being freed and eventually, Ruth began to emerge as a new self: herself. "I'm starting to live again—doing things I never thought I would do. Like a butterfly . . . I am experiencing a new and different life," Ruth explained. "George fulfilled me completely, but his leaving forced me to tune in within, and I like what I've found."

She's exploring new friendships in ways she rarely had before. "I started going out to lunch with friends and to movies during the day, 'our house' became 'my house,' and 'our friends' have become 'my friends'—it was all different now, but I was learning how to cope and live again," Ruth said. "Relationships with our couple friends now involve just me, but you know what— it's O.K. to be alone because now I know that I am never ever truly alone."

Death is no longer a fear for her—it's part of the stages of life which surround one in nature. "What one learns in the desperation of loss and death is one of life's most important lessons. By being alive, we are part of the mystery of life and order in the universe. The sense of union with loved ones is something that never leaves us. I know this to be true, because I feel as if I've learned how to take my husband and daughter into an inner sanctuary—wherever I go and wherever I am, they are here, within me, and their spirits will never go away."

Ruth's new life now embraces a deeper, profound sense of meaning—one that cherishes an eternal uniting of souls which is forever.

Fan Benno-Caris, 81

Dallas, Texas

Most days Fan is "up and at 'em" by 5 A.M. doing her "racewalk thing." This Olympian grandmother is one of the fastest, fittest women on earth—a title she intends to hold onto for years to come. "I expect to be the fastest racewalker on the planet when I'm 100," Fan exclaimed. "I'm going to keep moving no matter what! I may be getting older, but I'll never be old."

Recently ranked number three in the world, Fan gets places fast, especially considering she didn't even start this activity until she was 70. Inspired by a demonstration at the Cooper Institute, Fan remembers deciding that racewalking was the thing for her and immediately set her sights on striving to become a national champion. "It must be hereditary . . . my dad was very active and walked all the time. And I don't have any aches and pains, so I must be doing something right!"

Evidently she is, because after only two months she won her first of six (and counting) consecutive Texas State 1500 Master Racewalking Championships, and qualified for Nationals. "I remember being so excited winning my first medal, but now motivating others to walk and feel better is my real goal," Fan said. "It can make such a big difference in improving one's quality of life . . . and I want to share this message with as many people as I can."

Since she has won almost every award the sport has to offer, she has also become something of a celebrity and popular speaker in the process. Fan likes to speak because it enables her to encourage others to try walking, too. "I think we should take the word exercise out

of the dictionary and replace it with m-o-v-e, move. It doesn't matter how much or how far, the most important thing is to just do it every day!"

Fan's been on the move most of her life. She danced and played tennis when she was younger and even learned how to swim at the age of 60, but her accomplishments as a racewalker are far and above what she is most proud of.

"Of course, my husband, children, grandchildren, and great-grandchild are my support team and the joy of my life. But everyone needs something to reach for, something that keeps life exciting and provides goals to shoot for! I don't see what age has to do with that, because if you don't have something that excites you, that you enjoy doing, that's when depression can set in, and then a whole new set of problems arise from there."

Fan believes one of the best things about racewalking, or just walking in general, is that just about anybody can benefit by doing it—anywhere, anytime, and at any pace. There is nothing more natural than walking, and it's just as relaxing as it is good for you. "There are three styles of walking," Fan said. "Regular walking—like strolling, not working for speed; power walking— pumping the arms with each stride for more intensity; and racewalking—with a definite heel-to-toe stride form specifically for speed."

But regardless of the style, walking is unquestionably a great way to move the body. In fact, many doctors prescribe walking as a preventive treatment for back pain, as well as for weight control and lowering blood pressure and cholesterol levels.

"I know I've lived 81 years . . . but I don't feel 81 years old!" Fan laughed. "I'm not old; in fact, I may be one of the few who really looks forward to getting older so I can get up into that next age bracket for competitions!"

Fan's philosophy about aging seems to be right on target. She by no means believes age has to be an endpoint, but instead believes aging should be viewed as a continuation of life. Without this type of outlook, Fan feels too many people retire without any real plans for what they want to do and then somehow give themselves permission to do nothing—which she believes is the fastest way to get old.

"There's a definite difference between aging and getting old: we can't necessarily stop ourselves from aging and growing older . . . we just don't have to get old!"

Willa Billmeyer, 77

Encinitas, California

The yoga contortions Willa Billmeyer put her body into as a "senior citizen" were simply amazing! The feats she has accomplished since then are equally incredible. With a seemingly boundless supply of energy that she credits mostly to good health, Willa also admits that it hasn't always been this way.

"Twenty years ago, I had every type of "itis" you could think of . . . arthritis, phlebitis, encephalitis and more," remembered Willa. "I knew I needed to change the direction of my health—and that's when I decided to try yoga. I'll never forget my first class—I couldn't even touch my toes! I don't know why I was so surprised, since I'd been sedentary for years."

Improve her health she did, and Willa credits much of it to yoga. It improved the circulation throughout her body, helped her lose twenty-five pounds, eliminated of all the "itis" symptoms, and today she feels fifteen years younger and totally reenergized.

With good health and energy on her side, Willa decided to embark on some new challenges and adventures. She started with a walk—but not just any walk. This one was up and down the Grand Canyon in a total of seventeen hours at the age of 62. At 70, she hiked the Maui Crater in Hawaii, a 6,000-foot descent over 2.5 miles. Next was Australia's Ayers Rock, an incredible 80-degree climb that required her to physically pull herself up with upper-body strength during parts of the ascent. Willa says it was unquestionably the hardest thing she had ever done, but it was an accomplishment worth the challenge.

Willa's husband, Al, is equally amazing and one of her greatest challenges. "He retired at 80, is back at work today at the age of 83, and still does absolutely everything wrong!" Willa laughed. "He doesn't exercise or worry much about his diet and he continues to get away with it!"

Her most recent quest is returning to what she has always loved, dancing. Willa has taken up a new form, tap, and performs with a semiprofessional group—thoroughly enjoying the physical and mental challenge of learning all the routines. Her instructor is 80—with a heart pacemaker—so Willa's continually inspired by what's possible with age.

"My motto is, have a wonderful time with life. Never let age get in the way of a new challenge or adventure, because that's what keeps life interesting!"

"Banana" George Blair, 84

Cypress Gardens, Florida

The doctor's exact words were, "You won't be able to water-ski again, George, and certainly never barefoot." But those words also sparked the drive in George that makes him so unique. He's a legend, an inspiration, and is considered the international ambassador of water-skiing and barefooting.

George skis fast, often, and thinks it's a heck of a lot of fun. He was the first person to water-ski on all seven continents, which earned him a place in *The Guinness Book of World Records* at age 74. He was inducted into the American Water Ski Hall of Fame at age 76, and was the barefoot-jumping recordholder from age 69 to 76. Today he still performs, as he has for thirty-three years, in the ski show at Cypress Gardens, the longest-running entertainment show in the world—and the grandest water-skiing display ever.

"Barefooting is a contact sport, so there is the risk of injury, particularly when you're going 35-40 MPH and crash against the water," said George, describing his trade. "Barefooting is extreme . . . but I'm the king of hard hits," he claimed. "I've had a few nasty falls that have resulted in injuries, but nothing will stop my 'just do it' attitude, including a doctor who says I can't. 'Can't' just doesn't exist in my world."

His first experience with barefoot water-skiing came at the age of 46, but George didn't start competing in tournaments until he was 64. Since then, he's become an inspiration to people of all ages. "It's amazing to see all

the mail I get, and I always get such a kick out of the young kids who tell me they just hope they'll still be able to walk when they get to be my age! And to those who say I'm too old to be doing this, I tell them they're the ones missing out on all the fun!"

But George is not just about water-skiing. He's also a self-made millionaire, businessman, philanthropist, art connoisseur, actor, photographer, world traveler and musician . . . all as an octogenarian. His zest and zeal for life is due to his "no barrier" lifestyle—which continues to make George one of life's most interesting characters.

Recently clad in his bright yellow wetsuit, yellow sunglasses, sandals, and toting a banana-yellow long-board, George took up surfing, too! It was on his "to do" list as an activity he'd always been curious about, so why not give it a try? That's just part of his style. Amazingly, but typical of George's athleticism and water-sport agility, he even stood up on his very first try! "I love to feel the wind in my face and the energy rush through my body by trying new things. I learned how to snow-board at the age of 75, surf at 83, and my latest kick is racecar driving because I do love to go fast!"

Proving you're never too old to try something new, George joined the Skip Barber Racing School and ful-filled a dream of racecar driving. "Driving the racecar also proved to me that my mind and body still work as well as they did when I was 70—or 22 for that matter . . . so at 84, what's age got to do with it?" It's the fun, expe-rience, and exhilaration of a new challenge which makes life interesting to me . . . and if it involves going fast, you can definitely sign me up!"

To say George has left an impression on this earth is an understatement. If you were wondering where the nickname "Banana" George comes from, it's not just his bright yellow wetsuit, cars, phones, houses, and boats—he gives away more than three tons of Chiquita bananas every year, too! George believes they are quite possibly nature's most perfect food because they're loaded with vitamins, minerals, water, and have lots of energy-enhancing qualities.

So if it's energy you're after, take it from George, "stay curious, be active, have fun, eat bananas, and make the most of each and every day."

Helen Boardman, 100

Schaumburg, Illinois

When you reach the age of 100, there's a lot of curiosity as to what your secret might be. If you ask Helen how she did it, she'll tell you she doesn't know. But it might not be just one thing that leads to longevity . . . it may be several things . . . and Helen seems to have them all!

"Just last night I performed in a comedy play—so I stay very active, don't let things bother me, keep a positive attitude, eat right, and don't take any vitamins or medications, except for a daily aspirin. Plus I'm totally in love!" she exclaimed.

Helen's a newlywed: she's only been married to Bill for the last three years. After being happily married for forty-five years, Helen never dreamed she would fall in love again . . . but as the saying goes, "never say never," and she readily admits she's as happy today as she's ever been in her life. "I thought I'd found the best in my first husband, Curtis, and by no means would I have ever believed this type of special relationship could happen twice in one lifetime, to the same person . . . but it did, so I guess I'm just one of the lucky ones!"

Helen and Bill met at the retirement community where they live, and agree that their relationship was "love at first sight." Both had lost their spouses, but neither one had ever anticipated remarrying. "We fell in love, plain and simple . . . and when that happens, you get married! It doesn't matter how old you are . . . if you're not too old to fall in love then you're not too old to get married, so that's exactly what we did!"

The fact that Helen was a 97-year-old bride was of no concern to her or her octogenarian fiance; however, their families' concern was another matter. "I guess you could describe them as skeptical, at first—both Bill's family and mine," remembered Helen. "But once everyone met each other and saw how true and genuine our love really was, both our families gave us their support, and when we were married in a local church they were all there!"

Family is important to Helen. She has three children, ten grandchildren and ten great-grandchildren, which is the reason why she wrote her memoirs entitled, *Ninety-nine and Counting*, to pass on to the next generations. "I love to read, write, and learn from books," said Helen. "I did book reviews for many, many years . . . but then this macular degeneration set in and I lost so much of my ability to see that life really became a challenge."

Today, Helen is able to continue reviewing books because "talking books" (books on audiotape) are now available from the Library of Congress. She also can use a special machine, similar to a closed-circuit television, which magnifies type to a size that enables those with conditions like hers to keep reading.

"I always encourage people with vision difficulties to try books on tape . . . some do, while others prefer to do nothing . . . but it's their choice. I think what really matters is that there is an option, something that can help them stay involved even with their eyesight loss."

Helen's doctor says she's in excellent health. She's had both hips replaced, without any problem, and never once did her health get in the way of a good trip or adventure. "I've always loved to travel . . . in fact, we just got back from a trip to Spain and Portugal, and we honeymooned in Europe—Denmark, Holland, and England. If you want to see the world as I have, you can't let worn-out cartilage stop you. You've got to get that hip replaced so you can go on your way!"

Helen tries to keep life simple and focuses on the basics. She eats right, with lots of fruits and vegetables, but admits that dessert is her weakness, especially berry pie. And because she knows exercise is important, Helen can be seen doing her routine in the laundry room as she watches the washing machine. She says she stretches, bends, and walks but says it isn't a fetish . . . it's just something she knows has to be done.

"Perhaps the secret to living a long life is living long enough to know what you should do . . . and do it!" Helen exclaimed. "I've certainly lived long enough by now to know how to do it right . . . and I guess I am, because I'm healthy and happy!"

Woody Bowersock, 85

Laguna Hills, California

Woody decided early on that you have to retire *to* something, after you retire *from* something. He's not only found something he's good at, but something he gets better at each year. People say he looks the same as he did twenty years ago, and Woody says he feels as good, if not better, than he used to. So maybe his daily morning swim is more like diving into the proverbial fountain of youth, because Woody keeps improving with age . . . and he owns a host of masters swim world records to prove it.

"I've just been lucky, that's all. I've always been active, but I didn't get serious about swimming until the age of 64 or so, and since then it's just become a way of life for me. I swim every day and have for the past twenty years, because I knew I needed to find something to do in retirement."

Woody had always enjoyed swimming when he was younger, he just wasn't any good at it—or so he says. He laughs when people say he just preserved himself and saved his talent to use now, but there may actually be some truth to that belief. "I really wasn't developed enough when I was younger to compete seriously. But ever since I started swimming in retirement, I've been fairly competitive . . . even with tough competition, somehow I've been able to win."

Woody is recognized as one of the most prominent senior athletes in the country. He owns at least six masters swim world records in the freestyle and another world record in the 200-yard individual medley (butterfly, backstroke, breaststroke, and crawl). In addition to his personal accomplishments, Woody also competes regularly as an active team member of the Coast Masters. "In a recent meet our team broke three world records, and ironically enough, they were records we had set ourselves the year before, so there's the proof . . . you really can get better with age!"

Almost by chance, Woody fell back into swimming. While visiting Florida, he attended a Senior Olympics competition. He was not just a spectator—he became a participant and won the 440-meter run without any prior training. He also entered a swimming event, which he didn't win . . . but it did get him thinking that he would train for the following year and see what happened.

"I returned to California and started swimming regularly, not doing any real training regimen, just consistency, mostly. The next year, I went back to Florida, swam in the National Masters Championships, and placed sixth, fifth, fourth, third and second in my different events . . . so that inspired me to keep at it."

Woody is definitely into it now, some twenty years later, and he's recruited others to join him. When he first moved to Leisure World, he was the only master swimmer there. Now there are nine others, and three of them are members of the world-record-setting masters relay team. In fact, Leisure World is home to a number of top senior athletes, including the top three senior women swimmers in the world.

Although Woody has benefited greatly in terms of physical health and conditioning from swimming, there was a time several years ago when he felt so good that he may have overdone it a bit and wound up suffering a minor heart attack as a result. "It wasn't because of swimming; it was the combination of activities that set it off. I had competed in a three-day masters swim meet, where I swam hard and a lot . . . but I did well, too, because I took home thirteen golds and one silver. Anyway, my daughter wanted my wife and me to come up and visit, which was four-hundred miles away. So after the race I drove us there, felt O.K., and then stayed up playing cards with everyone, which in hindsight was probably not such a smart idea. I guess my body was more tired than I realized, because that's when I had the heart attack and ended up in the hospital."

Fortunately, however, Woody was in good physical shape because of his swimming, which enabled him to recuperate quickly. Before long he was back in the water again, and he's obviously recovered nicely, because that was ten years ago . . . and several swimming world records ago as well.

Without question, Woody's most challenging health problem occurred when he was 70. He was diagnosed with polymyalgia rheumatica, an excruciatingly painful illness that debilitated him for several months and prevented him from swimming competitively for almost a year. After the diagnosis, a doctor told him there was nothing Woody could do but take aspirin and rest. However, Woody sought out a specialist and through a variety of treatments his health improved.

"That was pain like I've never experienced before," Woody said. "I couldn't dress myself, nor raise my arm to scratch an itch without total pain. The only water work I did was in a ninety-degree rehabilitation pool, and I couldn't even swim across it! But I slowly got back at it and there was a happy ending besides just getting better . . .the first swim meet back after a year hiatus, I even won a medal!"

So Woody is a true champion in every sense of the word. He's overcome some difficult challenges, and he recognizes these hurdles are part of life, but he'll also tell you that swimming and being fit may have been the very things that actually enabled him to overcome the adversity he faced. At a time when many would have literally "thrown in the towel," Woody never would.

"I guess it's about attitude and how you feel about yourself," Woody said. "By being active with swimming I really didn't notice the aging process as much. So when I got sick, since I had felt so good before that, I knew I could feel that way again . . . and therefore, I had a healthy goal to shoot for."

Of course Woody has a lot to live for, with a great support team in his family. He's been married for sixty-three years to his wonderful wife, Vera. And when asked what the secret is to a happy, long marriage, he couldn't resist one of his favorite comedy lines: "The secret to a long marriage is a blind wife and a deaf husband!" he said with a laugh. But all kidding aside, he then said it's really about family, love, caring, and being together. "We are very family-oriented . . . with three daughters, seven grandchildren and thirteen great-grandchildren! We don't get to see each other often enough . . . sometimes a couple of months will pass, but then when we do gather, it's like no time has passed in between . . . we start up right where we left off."

Even though time ticks on and Woody keeps getting older, he says he just doesn't feel it. Maybe there really is something in that water, because Woody seems to just keep getting better with age.

Austin T. Brandenburg, 80

Middletown, Maryland

Who would have known that belonging to one of the first families in the neighborhood to own a television set would launch a unique career that would take Austin to new heights—literally.

Believe it or not, Austin is a professional antenna installer. He climbs towers as high as eighty to one-hundred feet—with no fear of heights, obviously, and even without safety devices! "I put up my first antenna for our family's first television set back in 1948," Austin said. "Then I got my second job when a neighbor got their first TV, and before long I found myself installing antennas for the local store that sold the TVs. The rest, I guess, is history."

Even though much of the area is now serviced by cable television, Austin is still busy. In fact, his competition even calls him to do their antenna work because they can't find anyone else willing to climb that high. "I wasn't always fearless of heights—it took a while, but now that I've been doing it for so long, I feel comfortable with my abilities and have little fear. The surroundings are always different. Some jobs are more challenging than others, but I figure, I've done it before so I can do it again. I try to concentrate on being careful. I really like what I do, too, so I don't see any reason to change it now that I'm 80!"

"I'm sure a lot of people think I'm just plain crazy! But I know what I'm doing and learned a long time ago how to do it right. You lock your legs around the pipes of the tower and just go slowly, methodically, and never, ever rush. Using the safety devices seemed more difficult to me because with every step, you have to hook and un-hook the belt. That messed up my rhythm and timing . . . so I choose to go without!" Austin has never fallen yet.

This mode of work and exercise does wonders for his body. Aside from an occasional arthritis flare-up, he has no aches and pains. "You've got to be in fairly good shape to do this kind of work. Raising and lowering a forty-five foot ladder by yourself takes a bit of muscle, and I guess I must have some because I can still do the work!"

Austin's work is his exercise and as far as his diet is concerned he says he eats whatever he wants because he's been able to maintain his 155-pound frame for a number of years. His supportive and loving family has also contributed significantly to his healthy life, and he is very proud of his two children and his fifty-six year marriage to his wife, Grace.

"I'm sure genes have had something to do with my longevity because both my parents lived into their nineties. I've always been active, too—I worked on my family's farm when I was younger, and still today enjoy physical labor that takes me outdoors."

He says he has no time for retirement—in fact, Austin says he'll never retire and will continue doing what he loves to do until he can't do it anymore. For this reason, it's easy to see why Austin is considered something of a legend in his land, and a very special man indeed.

Arnold Brilhart, 94

Vista, California

I magine spending seventy-five years in retirement . . . yes, seventy-five. As far as Arnold Brilhart is concerned, he retired at age 18, back in 1922. "My definition and philosophy about retirement is simply this: it's doing the things you want to do."

Undoubtedly it's this attitude and outlook on life that have contributed not only to his longevity but also to his continual involvement in the world around him.

At the young age of 93, Arnold's contributions continue today. He is a true legend, and although his name may not sound familiar, his musical accomplishments are many, and the list of people he performed with reads like a Who's Who in the Music Hall of Fame. He was a prominent player in music circles throughout the big band era. If you listened to the radio or watched any movies in the 1920s, 1930s or 1940s, you definitely heard his music. Arnold quickly became one of the most sought-after woodwind musicians of the time, performing in the California Ramblers Orchestra and on hundreds of radio shows, recordings, and motion-picture soundtracks for the NBC, ABC, and CBS studios.

He tells fascinating tales of events that transpired during his illustrious career. In 1924 Tommy and Jimmy Dorsey auditioned with the California Ramblers—the band Arnold was playing with. Arnold remembers their talent being extraordinary from the outset. The Dorseys were so good at their audition that the trombonist broke his instrument over his knee in utter disbelief.

Several years later, Arnold played with the Dorsey Brothers Orchestra. He recalls when a young lad by the name of Bing Crosby came to perform with their band. Unknown at the time, Crosby was paid about $15 to sing, compared to Arnold's $250 for the recording session. "I had to pay his green fees all the time, before Crosby made any money," Arnold said. That was O.K. since golf was an important part of Arnold's life. In fact, he can tell you stories about playing golf with Bob Hope, George Burns, and even Babe Ruth!

But it is Arnold's music career that is so incredible. He made more than thirty thousand recordings, at times played fifteen to twenty radio shows a week, and sat first alto chair alongside Louis Armstrong, Benny Goodman, Charlie "Bird" Parker, Xavier Cugat, and Jack Benny.

Today Arnold does consulting, research, and testing, for the company he founded in 1939, which manufactures reeds and mouthpieces for woodwind instruments. He believes being involved with things one is passionate about is key to success at any age.

"When you get to be 90, people think you're done. I'm thinking about what I'll be doing ten years from now! Old is not a number . . . it's a way of thinking.

When you stop growing, experiencing, and trying new things, you can get stuck in a rut and that's how you get old. So if you believe that's an automatic with age, then you're destined to get old real fast."

Arnold still has many interests in his life. He enjoys good health, independence, and has the charm, personality, spirit, and drive of someone you would guess to be half his age. "I have a positive outlook and keep myself involved," said Arnold. "I walk fast, have few aches or pains, follow a good vitamin program, and am very happy because I enjoy life!"

Sister Madonna Buder, 67

Spokane, Washington

While some people look around the starting line to size up their competition at the Ironman triathlon, still others look around in hopes of again seeing Sister Madonna. She is known as one of the most inspirational woman athletes ever, is considered among the top women's Ironman athletes, and is always referred to as undoubtedly one of the most faithful.

Sister Madonna is not your typical Catholic nun, nor is she your typical athlete who grinds and trains in almost obsessive ways. As one of the top women athletic performers, particularly for her age, she views her exercise and competition as a form of living prayer . . . a blessing, she says, which has been granted to her from above.

"Every day is a form of prayer for me," Sister Madonna shared. "It's a blessing to be alive and there is more to life than what merely just exists on the surface. Life has much deeper meaning than just going through the motions, which is why I feel so blessed to have my faith, which provides me with this understanding."

Sister Madonna applies this philosophy to everything she does, and one of the things she does is triathlons—athletic competitions that involve running, biking, and swimming. It is all done on the same day, back-to-back—a singular test of human endurance. She has an amazing eleven finishes at the original Ironman triathlon, held annually in Kona, Hawaii, and she holds the age-group record. Yet there's something very different about Sister Madonna's approach to these achievements, which is undoubtedly part of her secret to success.

"My training and participation are a tribute to my faith," Sister Madonna stated. "I cease to take anything as dogmatic . . . in fact, if anything, I believe it isn't. If it's not felt deep down inside, interiorized, then there's really no sense in owning it, regardless of what it is. Whether it's faith or training, you practice what you preach. The people who go to mass every morning and then think they've done their daily duty are an example. If they don't put those thoughts and prayers into daily action, then they really haven't taken to heart what they've just experienced in church . . . they're just going through the motions, not living them out."

Sister Madonna says morning mass is the way she "jump-starts her day," and she keeps the beliefs and spirit with her during her biking, swimming, and running workouts. She refers to this as 'intentionality', which she gives to anything she does, and by attaching her faith to everything she does, it becomes more valuable and meaningful to her.

"Running and biking are part of God's gift . . . he's given me the strength and ability to perform at these levels. By looking at it from this perspective, you see the bigger picture. It becomes a form of prayer for me, it's the intention behind the action, and it's actively living this blessing that makes the real difference."

People look forward to seeing her at the starting line, and she believes this has now become just another reason for her to keep on participating. Prior to a race, fellow competitors often ask her for a blessing, and she is always happy to oblige. Race directors are also pleased when they see she has entered their event because she miraculously seems to bring good weather.

"'A winner never quits and a quitter never wins' is part of my philosophy. I've had my share of injuries and crashes, but I live my life in a very determined sort of way. I'm here to make the best of every day, and I always will." Sister Madonna applies this attitude to all areas of her life. Although she was active growing up, she didn't even start running seriously until the age of 48, and that was in hand-me-down shoes.

After only five short weeks, she entered herself in the 8.2-mile Bloomsday Run in her hometown. Although it was difficult, she persevered nonetheless, and had faith she could do more. So she set her sights high and strived to complete a marathon before she turned 50.

"The well-known Boston Marathon was the goal for me, but as it turned out, I was 52 when I first ran it— probably the first Catholic nun to ever do so. Then I heard about these tri-events, with the bike, run, and swim—a marathon was crazy enough, but this took the cake as far as physical endurance goes."

Faith is what fuels her and enables her to continue pursuing new goals. And it is this same faith that Sister Madonna applies to her perspective on aging. In fact, she often laughs out loud when people ask her age or make a big deal about what she does because of her age. She thinks age has little to do with anything anyone does—it's what they believe in that really matters.

"I'm just doing my thing, living each day to the fullest," Sister Madonna said.

"Once you start thinking about age and basing whether or not you should do something on how old or young you are . . . then you're headed for real trouble.

If it's only about age, I probably would have given this all up by the time I turned 60. There's more to it than that . . . it must be part of God's plan, because here I still am!"

Whatever it is that moves her, it's obvious that she's guided by faith, which serves as an inspiration to her and others and helps them understand part of God's plan. It's the power of prayer and spiritual beliefs that really enables everyone to cross life's finish line.

Bob "Burnsy" Burnside, 66

Palm Desert, California

Bob "Burnsy" Burnside is barely a senior as qualified by age, and he certainly doesn't come close to resembling the image of a person taking it easy in his later years. "Retirement has nothing to do with sitting on the front porch, rocking your life away," Burnsy said. "In fact, I think retirement finally gives us the chance to go out and do it all . . . now we get our time to do what we want."

Of course, few would probably choose to spend their time the way Burnsy does, but "to each his own", as the saying goes. A world-class bodysurfer still competing and winning to this day, he is a grand champion who has never lost the edge.

"Pushing myself has always been my style, and I'm certainly not going to stop now," Burnsy said. "I like being on the edge . . . that rush of adrenaline you get when you really challenge yourself. It's a definite rush and something I continue to quest after. I guess the only difference now is that when I'm hanging on the face of a twenty-five foot wave, I insist on having a shoulder—an escape plan—a window to go out. I don't just insanely attack the wave anymore . . . I have more of a game plan now, and that has definitely come from years of experience . . . or wisdom, if you will."

Keeping himself in tip-top physical shape is also part of his plan, and he strongly believes that this has had a direct effect on the aging process . . . or perhaps the lack of it, in his case.

"I think it's about being active . . . anything active, just do it," Burnsy said. "Otherwise the aging thing is going to set in. I know there are people just as content being couch potatoes; they've never been active their entire lives and are perfectly happy with that. But at the same time, you also see those who maybe have been fairly sedentary most of their lives who do go out there, make a change, and reap the health benefits of doing so."

Burnsy's workout routine consists of a good balance of the three S's: swim, stretch, and strength. As a competitive bodysurfer, swimming is obvious, but the importance of stretching and strength training is a very close second. "You have to keep the muscles, joints, and tendons loose and flexible for range of motion, which is what the stretching provides. And the strength training with light weights and high repetitions keeps everything strong."

He doesn't understand why more older adults don't exercise, especially with the amount of research over the last several years touting the benefits of activity, particularly as we age. Performed regularly and consistently, physical activity may be one of the single most important elements in reversing the decline so often associated with, and accepted as, a normal, inevitable aspect of the aging process.

"I would think that people, regardless of how old they are, would value their bodies enough to take care of them and recognize that they owe it to themselves to do what it takes for good health. They can make a difference by doing so."

This is where the power of the mind so often plays a role: if you believe your later years to be a time of decline, then they will be. On the other hand, if you believe your later years to be a time of good health and vitality, you are more likely to take the proper lifestyle steps necessary to incorporate those activities into your daily life. "I definitely think aging is a mental trip," Burnsy said.

"For me, there are no excuses to quit; you've got to be mentally tough and keep yourself active just like at any other time in your life."

Burnsy seems to do a good job of keeping it all in perspective. When he talks about diet he doesn't think you have to be a fanatic, but he does agree that it's important to watch your intake or at least be conscious of it. He recognizes that stress can also be a problem if it's not kept in check and believes it's always best to be positive and optimistic about things—at least it helps make you feel better. Burnsy also sees nothing wrong with naps. Rest is important, and he believes that some people don't get enough good rest, which can contribute to a host of health problems.

Of course, for Burnsy there is also the issue of desire, particularly when you're talking about continuing to compete in youth-dominated bodysurfing. It's just another reason why he keeps himself in such good physical shape—age won't slow him down. It's a spirit that motivates him in other areas of his life, too—that eternal search for the rush and the ultimate edge.

"I think I stay young because I continue to go out and do fun things I enjoy," Burnsy said. "Age doesn't, won't, and shouldn't ever have anything to do with changing that."

Jeanne Calment, 122 (1875–1997)

Arles, France

She holds a place in history as the oldest person in the world. Jeanne Calment was born on February 21, 1875 and died August 4, 1997, at the age of 122. She lived a good life—and indeed a long life—a life in which she was "never bored," in her words. Jeanne experienced the invention of the telephone and radio, was fourteen when the Eiffel Tower was completed in 1889, and even remembered meeting Vincent Van Gogh.

Yet how she experienced her later years was as extraordinary as the life she lived. She took up the sport of fencing at 85 and still rode her bike at 100. She powdered her cheeks with a dab of red rouge and only quit smoking and having her daily glass of wine at 117. Though blind and nearly deaf at the time of her death, Jeanne remained spirited and mentally sharp.

Unaware that she would live so long, Jeanne sold her apartment when she was 90 to a local lawyer, on an annuity system under which he would inherit it after she died. But after paying out for thirty years, the lawyer died at age 77 without ever taking possession. Jeanne outlived her husband, brother, daughter, and even her grandson; she left no direct descendants.

Her birthday parties were like national events, with well-wishers from all over the world asking her secrets to long life. Always gracious, many fondly remember how Jeanne showed her appreciation. On her 100th birthday, she rode her bicycle all over town and thanked everyone who helped her celebrate!

Jeanne Calment will always be remembered as a true model of hope and inspiration to all.

Thomas Cannon, 72

Richmond, Virginia

He is perhaps one of today's greatest philanthropists, not because he has lots of money to give away, but because he doesn't . . . and he still gives. Living spartanly on a postal worker's salary, Tom has distributed nearly $100,000 of his hard-earned funds and retirement income, in $1,000 increments, mostly to strangers, in an effort to convey to the public a message of brotherhood and caring.

"I don't do this for attention, because frankly I don't really care what other people think about me. But I'll have to admit, it's inspiring to see others receive my message and be inspired by my actions. That matters much more to me than all the attention I get just for doing what I think is right. It validates that this is important."

Tom's generous gift-giving began in 1972 when he and his family lived in a tiny kerosene-heated home in a poor neighborhood. A young man living next door was legally blind, and Tom read in a newspaper about a new device which could enhance the vision of people with the young man's condition. It cost $1,000, and Tom immediately decided to buy it for the boy—but was politely refused. The young man had a support network of family and friends and said he was suited nicely to his way of life.

Although Tom's initial donation was declined, it planted the $1,000 gift idea in his head, because since then he's given away numerous gifts to unsuspecting people. Sometimes he finds them by reading the newspaper, and many try to find him—letters come in from all over the world addressed to "the man with the heart of gold."

His prerequisites for determining who should receive gifts are rather basic: has the person made a significant contribution to the community or his fellow man? Does the person have a traumatic hardship? He does not reply to correspondence soliciting money because his message is absolutely, positively not about just giving away money. "I do what I do as a matter of routine spiritual principle. I'm implementing the philosophy of the brotherhood of man under the fatherhood of God by personally demonstrating that the finer qualities of the human soul—not money—represent the ultimate values in life."

Tom says he gets tremendous satisfaction and inspiration from all the letters he receives. One he remembers receiving recently was from a woman who said she had become very pessimistic about the human race until she heard what Tom was doing. It changed her whole perspective. She simply thanked Tom for caring, giving a damn, and making a difference.

"Her letter reinforced the primary purpose of my philanthropy, which is really to be upbeat about our fellow humans," Tom said. "She represents how many people feel depressed about man's inhumanity to his fellow man. It's hard to stay positive when we see all the cruelty and hatred going on in our world—murders and racism that bombards us every day in the media, day in and day out. It really gets to you—or at least it gets to those of us who care and actually give a damn," he concluded.

Tom believes it's more important than ever for everyone to do what they can to try to make the world a better place. Examples of those he has helped are the teenager from a poor family who found a wallet with $40 on the schoolbus and turned it over to the driver, the group of teenagers who rescued a drowning horse, or the Junior Woman's Club who enriched the lives of underprivileged children by taking them to parks and museums. It's about people caring and doing for others.

People have cared a lot about what Tom's doing, too, because donations poured in from those who wanted to repay him for his years of kindness after learning about his own personal hardship. A columnist for his local newspaper who often chronicled Tom's good deeds, once wrote about the story behind the scenes. Born into poverty, Tom never earned more than $32,000 a year and has continued his philanthropy on a retirement income of $16,800. Much of that goes to pay the medical bills of his wife of fifty-one years, Princetta, who has suffered two strokes, is legally blind, bedridden, and unable to care for herself.

"I never would have accepted the donations if I had been single, but Princetta's needs came first. I could not in good conscience turn down their generosity, because it enabled our family to move to a nice neighborhood and a home with central heat, which is much better for my wife's health now."

In addition to tending to his philanthropy, Tom serves as the primary caregiver for his wife, eighteen hours a day. He sleeps on the floor by her bed in case she needs him. This experience and Tom's philosophy about life have definitely influenced his perspective on aging. First and foremost, he believes there is far too much fear of growing old and dying in our society, and he says this acute fear actually accelerates the aging process.

"The old geezers who are always whimpering and whining, saying things like, 'I'm not what I used to be,' are unwittingly and unknowingly transmitting mental commands to their body cells to hasten the aging process, to die," Tom said. "Only the physical body—the vehicle, the earthly garment—ages chronologically. The soul entity, in dwelling and expressing itself through the physical body, is beyond the aging of earthly matter. It is ageless."

Tom doesn't worry too much about the aging process because he's too busy living and doing for others, and he believes it's simply a natural phenomenon. But human kindness is not—goodness happens by design, and it's obvious that the world needs more people like Tom Cannon, whose extraordinary generosity will continue to reward those who do good and will hopefully inspire others to make a difference, too.

Joe Clapers, 74

Baltimore, Maryland

The doctors said they had never seen a senior like him before, and if Joe has his way, they won't be seeing him again anytime soon. Joe claims he has always suffered from a "white coat syndrome" so he keeps himself healthy through an exercise regimen few at his age can do.

"My buddies from the gym and I were just on TV last week, a live shot of us all working out, and I benched 315—the same weight I lifted when I was 50! At the gym we're known as the 'Old Guys' since we're all over 63 . . . but the young guys think what we do is great and hope to do the same thing when they get to be our age. I guess maybe we are an inspiration."

Clapers provides much of the inspiration—often referred to as "The Rev," due to his devout faith in Christianity, good attitude, and ability to motivate others. Faithfully, Joe and his buddies can be found pumping iron three days a week in such massive quantities of weight that no one would dare call them seniors. But they are, and claim they are proud of both their age and what they can still do.

"Our age is about the only thing that designates us as seniors," Joe said. "I may be getting older, but I feel great and have virtually no health problems . . . so exercise must keep you from aging. I'll bet we outlift 90 percent of the people in the gym, so I really don't think age has anything to do with it . . . we just keep doing what we've always done, and it seems to work!"

Joe is also quick to add that as much as he believes in the "use it or lose it" philosophy, he encourages those just getting started to get instruction, begin slowly, and never do exercises that hurt. The ninety-minute routine Joe and his buddies do however, makes you hurt just thinking about it. They do three sets each of warmup bench presses (160 to 185 pounds), bench presses (up to 315), decline bench presses (up to 325), dumbbell bench presses (90 pounds in each hand), tricep bench presses (up to 160), lat pulldowns (up to 150), tricep pushdown exercises (up to 200), barbell curls (up to 110), and cross-cable flys (up to 80).

"It's not just about lifting," Joe stated. "A well-rounded routine enables you to continue doing it on a regular basis, which is what really keeps you healthy. Equally important is the cardiovascular workout—to build a strong heart. I walk three miles a day up and down the hills in my neighborhood, or on the treadmill in my den if the weather's bad. Combined with my daily 400 to 500 sit-ups, this has helped keep the doctor away!"

He claims he has no age-related conditions such as arthritis, has never been sick or broken a bone, has kept his weight the same for the past fifteen years, never has headaches or bodyaches, and has arms that resemble Popeye's. He did have some trouble with his knees, so he switched from running to walking. Last year he had an angioplasty to clear out an artery that was 80 percent blocked, but he was back at the gym and on the treadmill within a few weeks.

"As great as I feel and as normal as my routine seems to me . . . you just don't see that many older adults doing this. The gym scene has really been primarily promoted for the young . . . but I think it's the gym thing that *keeps* you young. If I stopped this, I probably would begin to age."

47

Joe believes much of his strength ultimately comes from God. "I say the joy of the Lord is my strength, and a scripture in the Bible says, 'The glory of a young man is his strength and the beauty of an old man is his gray hair.' Therefore, the way I see it, I've got a young body with gray hair, so I guess that means I'm beautiful!"

Joe's spiritual convictions have also instilled a strong sense of purpose in his life and a true understanding of the importance of doing for others. He goes to church every morning to help pray for those who have made prayer requests, and through this process he has realized just how blessed he is.

"I realize and appreciate the strength I've received from God and I've allowed the Holy Spirit to guide me, which has resulted in an abundant flow of blessings. So if I can continue to help, and live my life as an example or inspiration to others . . . that's a good thing that has nothing to do with age."

Anne Clarke, 88

Carol Stream, Illinois

Although Anne's story starts out like most, it certainly doesn't end like most. Of course, Anne does a lot more finishing in her life than most people and claims the day she finishes last will be the day she may consider staying home . . . but it hasn't happened yet, and it does not appear it will anytime soon.

Up until the age of 69, Anne Clarke says she led a totally sedentary life. If it weren't for a dead car battery that prompted her to walk the one-mile distance to her teaching job, she would have missed out on all she has achieved since then, including feeling better at 80 than she ever did at 50!

"I really did start feeling better the more I walked, and that's how I began making it a regular part of my day," Anne said. "I know a lot of people don't believe something as simple as walking can make such a difference in a person's health, but it really can and does, especially if you were like me and had been sedentary for so long."

Anne started out walking gradually but regularly, and she strongly believes that the benefits of exercise occur when activity becomes a daily part of life. It did for Anne, because before long she began picking up speed, and eventually added running to her repertoire. The steps she has taken led her to places Anne never would have dreamed she would be, including being considered a world-class runner and one of the finest senior athletes in the country.

Her first competition was a 10K (6.2 mile) event at age 69 that she ran in sixty-nine minutes. Since then, Anne has competed in more than five hundred races world-

wide and holds more than fifty-four national running records in her age group for events ranging from 5Ks to marathons. She has competed in an amazing eight marathons, her last at the age of 81 in Chicago, where she set both a national and world record for her age group.

Her battles with health have been and will continue to be a challenge, but she also realizes the condition she might have been in if she didn't have this as her "medication." "When I was in my fifties, I had lots of aches and pains due to arthritis. I was taking lots of pills, which I really didn't like. But when I started exercising it seemed to get better and now I'm free of all medications. Just natural vitamins and running and/or walking: that's my daily prescription!"

Anne continues to pass along what she has learned by also teaching exercise classes four times a week at a two local retirement communities. She also gets inspiration from a 103-year old woman who she sees walking two miles a day—just more proof that it's a secret to keeping going!

"I do believe in this . . . it certainly has worked for me, and although I do not preach it to others, I do encourage people to give it a try and see what happens," Anne said. "Some limitations do come with age, but I also believe a positive attitude and a sense of doing something constructive can make a difference."

Anne reflected on the recent loss of her husband, Hamilton Clarke, the true love of her life with whom she spent sixty-three years and misses immensely. "Sometimes I get depressed from the grief of missing him. But I also know that he would want me to keep this up, so that inspires me to keep on going. I'm doing this both for me and in the loving honor and memory of him, too."

Jack Costanzo, 70

Chula Vista , California

If you think young, you stay young: that's the motto Jack, a.k.a. "Mr. Bongo," patterns his life by. He's one of the great legends who introduced bongo drums to American music, and those who've had the privilege of hearing him perform recently, recognize he hasn't lost a beat—his passion for his art has not wavered with age.

He's been described as being to the bongo drums what Babe Ruth was to baseball. He's a true icon. His forty-year career included playing with the greats: Elvis Presley, Jerry Lewis, the Stan Kenton Jazz Orchestra, and Nat King Cole. He even had jam sessions at the home of Marlon Brando and on the movie set of *Guys and Dolls*.

"I love what I do, and have all my life," Jack said. "I think that's how I've kept myself so youthful all these years. Music is ageless, so if I stay involved with it, then maybe that's how I'll beat the age game!"

Jack thinks aging is a pain in the derriere, plain and simple. Perhaps one of the reasons for this is the youth-dominated medium in which he performs. The speed, fervor, and passion he brings to his work are due to his love for music, and age has nothing to do with that. But when you see and hear him play, you realize it is also his age that makes him so unique. In fact, if more people knew his actual age, there's little doubt they would be that much more impressed with his extraordinary talent.

"There's no doubt in my mind that I am a better player today than I was when I was younger. I've learned so much more, and fortunately my faculties have stayed stable, which has enabled me to continue to improve."

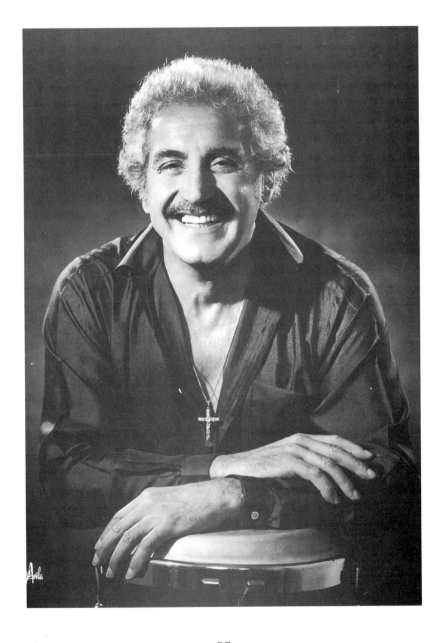

Playing the bongo or congo drums is quite a physical activity, one that requires athleticism and stamina. In fact, Jack often refers to the fast-paced music he performs as a good workout. And although he walks regularly, it is perhaps his triweekly trips to the gym to work out his upper body, which really may be contributing to his ability to keep up this pace.

"I think I must have good genes, too, because I have to admit, I've not really focused on a good diet until the last sixteen years or so. Of course, I've always been relatively healthy . . . don't smoke, drink, or take drugs, and even though I usually have a late-night schedule, I always make sure I get enough good rest."

Whatever it is, it appears to be working, and Jack has no plans to change this gig anytime soon. In fact, he is currently putting together a new band to begin a tour in Europe. Jack also credits his mother's words of wisdom: "What's in your mind shows in your physical," he said. "So if you think young, you'll stay that way. And if you are lucky enough to do what you want, which I always believed I could, then you'll wonder like I often do, what's age got to do with it?"

Ray Crawford, 73

Encinitas, California

I t can be a scary thing to have your father die at 61 and your brother at 51, both of heart attacks—and to know that heart problems are often hereditary. Ray did inherit a health problem, but he took control and believes he knows what it takes to survive and be healthy. "Exercise, exercise, exercise . . . I preach it like I would out of a Bible because I know it saved my life, and I believe it can save other people's, too."

Ray was relatively active most of his life, and he recognizes that if he hadn't been he might not be here today. He regularly rode his bike or walked to work, was an avid skier who swooshed down fourteen-thousand-foot mountains, and never once remembers feeling any symptoms of angina.

"When I turned 50, my plan was to retire at 55 in perfect health, but when I went in for my physical exam, that's when we discovered all my clogged arteries. The scariest part was not experiencing any of the traditional symptoms that would indicate there was a problem, but there obviously was, because the doctor basically intimated that I had no more than five years to live!"

As it turned out, Ray has lived considerably longer than originally expected because he was in such good physical shape—it literally saved his life. In fact, he has survived seventeen additional years with medications, maintaining his active lifestyle, and by watching his diet.

"I'm not a guru when it comes to diet . . . I do like cheese and occasionally pig out on chocolate, but it's the exercise component that has really made the difference."

Of course, the five-artery bypass surgery in 1991 (when Ray was 67) has played a part in his survival since then too. "I was back swimming at the YMCA within three weeks of my surgery. And I can tell you honestly that I feel like my body is in the best shape of my life right now, for the first time ever . . . even after all of that, probably because I have to take care of myself . . . and you bet I do."

Ray credits swimming and running as part of the reason for his survival, and he's pretty darn good at them too. He has won numerous medals in both events while competing in the Senior Olympics. In fact, Ray recently medaled in every track and field event he entered and also in the 400-meter freestyle swim.

"If I live, I want to be healthy; it's just that simple. The competitions have been fun and motivating, but it's really about keeping in shape to stay alive. Since my bypass, this regimen is essential for my longevity, and I know it."

Ray also believes it's more than just taking care of himself. He also takes care of others, and just received his five-thousand hours-of-service award for twenty years of volunteering at the Veterans Administration Hospital.

"It's a wonderful feeling to do things for others—it's healthy, and it makes you feel happy. Life really isn't that complicated: take care of yourself, do for others, and live your life by example. If doing that changes, motivates, or inspires something positive in others, then that is what life is really all about."

Hulda Crooks, 101 (1896–1997)

Loma Linda, California

A t age 100, she published her memoirs, *Conquering Life's Mountains*. The title refers to both the challenges of overcoming everyday life and Hulda's later-in-life passion: climbing the tallest and most challenging mountains. Nicknamed "Grandma Whitney" not only for her twenty-four climbs up Mt. Whitney, a 14,495-foot ascent that some refer to as "a human rite of passage," but perhaps more importantly because these climbs were all made between the ages of 66 and 91. In honor of Hulda's feats and to recognize her as the oldest woman to ever scale Mt. Whitney, a specific peak on Mt. Whitney was named Crooks Peak, in a ceremony that Hulda attended, via helicopter, at the age of 95.

She began her hiking adventures at the age of 54 as a means of solace after the death of her husband. She started with the San Bernardino Mountains' 11,502-foot Mt. Gorgonio, which she climbed about twenty times in preparation for the challenging Mt. Whitney. In addition to being the oldest to climb Mt. Whitney, Hulda was also the oldest to climb the 12,388-foot Mt. Fuji in Japan as well.

At the age of 72 Hulda discovered that jogging and running made climbing easier, so she introduced these activities into her regular exercise regimen. She even competed in the Senior Olympics at 82, running 1,500 meters in ten minutes and fifty-eight seconds, a world record for the 80 to 85 age group.

Still, at the age of 95 Hulda continued to walk two miles a day and often claimed good health doesn't just happen by accident—it has to be worked at. But she was also quoted as saying, "Exercise you enjoy does more good than exercise you do just because you think you have to. If you say 'I'm going to do this even if it kills me,' it just might, if you do it that way."

But Hulda's longevity was credited to more than just her exercise; it was also her religious faith. She once told a reporter that her mountain-climbing and running were her "high-altitude evangelism," aimed towards inspiring others to value physical health as a tool for good spiritual health.

There will always be mountains to climb along life's journey, and the spirit of Hulda Crooks will forever be there to help guide the way.

Mary Cunningham, 90

Buena Park, California

W hen you make plans for innovative birthday celebrations, by the time you reach the age of 90 the ideas seem to get more and more unique. "The sky's the limit" became the theme for Mary's day, which actually included a tandem skydive from 15,000 feet! "I've done just about everything else . . . so why not a parachute jump from a plane for my birthday? Oh! It was such a thrill. I loved every minute of it!"

Mary obviously has no fear of heights, since she's taken to the sky for other birthday celebrations, too, all in various parts of California. She rode a glider over the mountains in Hemet for her 70th, spent her 75th in a hot-air balloon over the Temecula Valley, and her 80th was a fun-filled day of roller-coasters at Magic Mountain.

"I thought a new birthday adventure was in order every five years, but now I think we should do it every year—so on my 91st, I'm thinking a white-water raft trip might be fun! "It'll be hard to top this . . . but I'm willing to give it a try! My friends think I'm a little nuts, but that's O.K.—somebody's got to do it. Most people know I'm pretty unpredictable and spontaneous, but that's what keeps life interesting."

Not all of her fun comes just from the air—her 85th birthday was spent driving through Glacier National Park in Montana. Mary admits she has a bit of the travel bug. She's been in almost all of the fifty states and believes her sense of adventure, continual going, doing, and having fun have definitely been key to her healthy aging.

The plan for her 90th birthday was a toss-up between a bungee jump and the parachute skydive, but while watching the bungee cord's jerking motion as it re-tracted, Mary liked the the gentle floating of the para-chute jump better.

"When I told my niece Jeanie and her husband Larry that I thought the skydive would be fun, they quickly went to work seeking out the best man for the job. They found him in Lake Elsinore, California, and although he admitted he'd never filled a request like mine, to his knowledge I am the oldest jumper ever!"

Although she's always been something of a daredevil, both Mary's family and the instructor were adamant that she get a doctor's clearance before she embarked on her latest endeavor. The doctor gave her a clean bill of health, and with a thumbs-up sign of approval he sent her on her way to be fitted for her birthday flightsuit.

"I got all gussied up in a brand-new outfit—a jump-suit with all the gear I needed for my birthday fun . . . a flight up and a jump down with a soft, safe landing," Mary said. "They coached me with training tips and most importantly demonstrated how, when, and where to pull the rip cord. They told me to smile, too, but I was worried I might lose my dentures! I wasn't scared at all though—in fact, I told jokes on the ride up. When I was ready to jump, I remember looking down and being absolutely amazed by all the houses we could see below."

Mary got a little extra special treatment for her jump: instead of taking the plane up to just 12,500 feet, they decided to take her 2,500 feet higher so she could enjoy the view and ride a little while longer—an extra seventy-second free fall, to be exact. "It was so peaceful, serene, and beautiful up there . . . you just can't imagine!" Mary said. "Plus there must have been two hundred people on the ground ready to greet me, all smiling and giving me a thumbs-up for a job well done—including a TV news crew."

Mary's family had notified the local news stations about the event in advance and were told that if it were a slow news day, someone might be sent to film it. It was a slow day, and Mary's birthday party was seen not only on the local news but all across the country and internationally as well. "Thank God for a slow news day!" Mary said. "We got calls from friends all over the place. Even my great-grandniece in Holland . . . I became a celebrity overnight! I just ate it up. It's beautiful when something so unexpected happens—it was a lot of fun!"

Birthdays will always be fun memories for Mary, who keeps a journal highlighting some of her fondest memories and special adventures, which she someday hopes to publish for her family. "I'll do that one of these days . . . when I'm old," Mary said. When asked when that would be and what old was—Mary simply shrugged her shoulders, smiled and said with a twinkle in her eye, "I don't know . . . but I'll let you know when I get there!"

Fran Daugherty, 78

Chula Vista, California

Once a teacher, always a teacher . . . and it is this philosophy that has enriched Fran's retirement, expanded her world, broadened her horizon, and even helped her overcome the grief of widowhood.

After spending thirty years as an elementary-school teacher, Fran had no plans to be idle in her retirement years. Yet within only four brief years of starting a whole new life, free of school bells with plans to travel all over the world with her beloved husband Emmett, it all came to an abrupt and tragic end when he died suddenly after returning from their evening walk.

"I had the most blissful and magical marriage anyone could hope for. It was absolutely heavenly . . . but it was unfortunately much shorter than I ever would have dreamed, and that is something you never prepare for or completely overcome."

Fran and Emmett were able to fulfill some of their travel plans during those four brief years. She also will be the first to admit that it was indeed their mutual love of travel, new experiences, and adventures that has enabled her to cope with his sudden death. "He once told me that if anything ever happened to him, he didn't want me to sit inside these four walls and grieve . . . he wanted me to continue traveling, learning, and sharing our dream. So that is what I've tried to do; as difficult as it was and still is, I know this is what he would have wanted. He's with me still and always will be . . . and it is my everlasting faith in God that has enabled me to believe this and feel eternally connected with him."

But it wasn't like that at first. Fran said it was as if she couldn't breathe without him. They were so close and his death was so sudden that she had no idea how she could possibly survive. She was in such a state of shock that it was like living in another world.

A variety of things helped Fran heal. Friends, faith, writing, and even a return to teaching were all beneficial. "A friend from my church who teaches Japanese in a local high school asked if I might be interested in tutoring some Japanese students in English as a second language," Fran said. "I had no background whatsoever in Japanese but felt it was something I could do. I've been doing it ever since, and that was more than seven years ago."

Fran became very close to one student in particular, and even "adopted" her in a non-legal sense and now has "grandchildren" as a result. The student enriched Fran's life, and the relationship was evidently mutual because Fran was invited to visit the young woman's family home outside of Tokyo. The cultural opportunity to live with her family was one of the most beautiful and extraordinary experiences of Fran's life.

Although her health has been a challenge, it only slows her down a bit—but she'll never let it get her down. "I take my daily walks and stay as active as I can . . . but I will never be idle . . . there's no time for that!"

Even with the empty spot in her life from the loss of her husband, she is thankful for all she does have, especially her faith,and the resulting connection with Emmett. Sometimes she feels like "Mother Nature and Father Time have formed a strong conspiracy against me," but she has no intention of letting them win. Although her body may be old, she's still young at heart. As a result, Fran's got the world in her hands.

Norton, 79, and Betty, 78, Davey

Oceanside, California

I magine biking 150 miles, running 30 to 40 miles and swimming 300 laps every week, all for the pure joy of fitness and competition. This is the "retirement" regimen of Norton Davey. And to think it has come to all this after a simple recommendation from his company's medical director to add a little exercise to his life some twenty-four years ago.

Since then Norton has become a testimony to athleticism at any age and a role model for a new generation of seniors finding that life can begin with retirement. He climbs some of the world's tallest mountains, including the 19,341-foot Mt. Kilimanjaro in Africa, runs marathons, and competes annually with the elite in his age group in one of the most challenging events known to man: the Ironman Triathlon in Kona, Hawaii. In fact, Norton is one of only two men in the world who have ever completed the Ironman after the age of 75, and he's competed in the event an amazing fifteen times in the past sixteen years!

The Ironman event begins with a 2.4-mile open-ocean swim followed by a 112-mile bike ride, and it ends with a 26.2-mile run—a mere sixteen-hour workout for Norton, all back-to-back in one day. He does it because he feels great and enjoys the competition.

Although he's unique, Norton says he tries to live his life as an example for others. "I noticed when I first started exercising—which I did by just walking and then running—three things happened. First and foremost, I felt better . . . not that I ever really felt bad, but I lost some weight and just felt great. Second, my vital signs improved, which also explains why I felt better, and third, I entered my first 10K race and got 'hooked' on competition."

Norton claims it was a slow process—he didn't just start doing all this overnight. It took time, obviously, to work up to the triathlon level. In fact, he remembers that when he first started swimming he could barely make the length of the pool, and as for running, he could barely walk around the block.

Most have heard about the health benefits of exercise, particularly with age, but few have the stamina to take on a feat like Norton's. However, that too may be changing, because he definitely has more company his age in competitions today than he ever had before. When he competed in his first Ironman at the age of 63, there were only four others over the age of 60. Since then he has been the oldest finisher in at least six Ironman events. In the 1997 event there were four others joining him in the 75-and-over age bracket, and more than fifty-five participants over the age of 60.

"The secret to aging is definitely out. To stay healthy, stay active, and to stay active, stay healthy! I believe our bodies are capable of more than we give them credit for, particularly as we get older, and if you commit to a safe, sensible exercise routine and good healthy diet . . . who knows how long we might be able to go!"

Norton has not done this all alone, however. He gives a lot of credit to his beautiful bride of fifty-five years, Betty, 78, who has continually supported his efforts. Betty also has maintained an active lifestyle, and after suffering a mild stroke she realized just how much of a role exercise has played in both her health and her re-covery process.

"I actually started exercising twenty-three years ago, at the age of 55, and have been very consistent in my rou-tine," Betty said. "I've pedaled more than 53,000 miles on my stationary bike, riding thirty minutes a day. I attend a "lite" aerobics class three times a week, followed by a stretch class. I lift light weights, two-to-three pound handweights two or three times a week and then on my 'off' days of no classes, I walk briskly for about forty-five minutes to an hour, totaling three to four miles."

Betty and her doctors will be the first to admit that it was this exercise routine that they credit not only for her speedy recovery but also the mildness of her stroke. She remembers the doctors—from her cardiologist and oph-thalmologist to her neurologist—all unanimously agree-ing that if Betty had not been in such good physical condition, her stroke would have been much worse.

Certainly exercise contributed greatly to her recovery, but Betty also credits years of healthy eating. She has been a vegetarian most of her life, serving lots of fruits, vegetables, and salads to her family over the years. And she also recognizes the role a balanced life and loving family have played in her good health and long life, too.

"I am both thankful and fortunate for all the good in my life," Betty said. "Loving parents who never put me down while I was growing up, a loving husband, family, and friends, as well as being a happy person with a good attitude and outlook on life have all contributed to how I am today. I'm proud of my age . . . in fact, on my 78th birthday I announced to my exercise class how energized and great I felt. My wish for them was to feel the same when they get to be my age!"

Together, Norton and Betty continue to be a team committed to helping others believe it's never too late to incorporate healthy behaviors into one's lifestyle and to benefit from them. They lead by example and are definitely an inspiration to follow.

Faye Davis, 80

Enid, Oklahoma

She has survived being a widow for twenty-eight years with no children, made it through two cancer diagnoses, still lives independently, and does her own housework and yardwork (except mowing). Faye has a home-based business, volunteers with her church, exercises daily, and celebrated her 80th birthday with a white-water raft trip in the morning, alpine skiing in the afternoon, and a business meeting in the evening!

To say Faye keeps herself busy is obvious, but it is her happiness factor that really should be measured. She is a delightful and inspiring woman who believes her positive attitude and faith have been the secret to her success. "Attitude has everything in the world to do with healthy aging. I like myself and what I'm doing. There are tough days and times, but the past is the past, so you might as well put negative thoughts aside because the future is ahead and you don't want the past to mess that up!"

Adventures and trying new things make life fun for Faye. Currently she's in the process of building her own Amway team after being a distributor of the products for the past twenty years. And it was while attending an Amway convention that she celebrated her 80th birthday in a most unique way. "We were in Colorado with a group of Amway people who were mostly in their fifties. They said they were going to 'float' down the river, and since it sounded like fun I decided to join them. Little did I know we were going to be white-water rafting . . . but I didn't back down, and I'm glad I didn't because I thought the white waters were absolutely the best!"

Later that afternoon, with a break in the meeting schedule, there was just enough time to fit in a little skiing. As Faye approached the ticket window, the cashier politely asked her age, and Faye, fearing she was too old to participate, was sure she was going to be turned away. Quite the contrary: she was given a complimentary ski pass in honor *of* her age and her birthday!

"People and laughter seem to be the secrets to my positive spirit and outlook on life," Faye said. "The special relationships I have with my family and friends make life worth living, and laughter is good medicine for the soul. Age seems to have little to do with it, so I'll never let it get in the way of anything I do!"

Frances Davis, 104

Nashville, Tennessee

Few people expected to see her driving the highways again after a policeman pulled her over at the age of 99. At 104 she's on the road again . . . this time, however, it's the information superhighway, and no cop will ever be able to stop her here.

"The sirens were going, and it was a frightful sight being pulled over like that, but he can't get me now because I do all my driving from home—on my computer and the Internet!"

It's true; this centenarian is computing instead of commuting, and she says it's a heck of a lot easier staying in touch with people by e-mail than messing with all those stamps. Although there are some friends she still writes to, mostly from her generation, she's got the rest of the world at her fingertips.

"My granddaughter gave me the computer for my 104th birthday because she thinks I can do anything and knows I'll always try! I thought it would be a fun new adventure—plus, I wanted to learn because I feel fortunate to be alive during this time of technology—and if it's here, you might as well use it. "

And use it she does. Frances enjoys learning and describes herself as a determined student. She goes online every day to leave electronic messages for her daughter as well as her six grandchildren and eleven great-grandchildren. She uses the computer to stay in touch with her church pastor, too, because she's no longer able to go to services and this enables Frances to stay connected.

"I'm surprised everyone is so fascinated at what I'm doing—there's been a lot of news coverage about me and my computer, so I should say I'm doing this to be famous!" Frances said. Although fame may have been the result, it certainly wasn't the intent. Frances is one who has always had a zest for life and a keen interest in people. Whether it's staying in touch with family or friends via the computer, getting together with her gal pals for bridge and lunch, or making a casserole for someone who needs it, Frances cares about others and is genuinely in love with life.

"I'm always trying to look ahead instead of looking back at what has been. I never thought much about living this long, but now that I'm here, I think I'll stay. I always keep busy with family, friends, and my faith, and maybe that's what it takes because I feel pretty great. I haven't worn glasses in twenty-plus years, and I only take three pills a day—a multivitamin, an aspirin, and my heart medicine."

Frances prides herself on her independence. She still manages her own affairs, makes all the decisions, takes care of the household bills and property taxes, and her grandson files the yearly income taxes. "My mind still works, so I continue to use it," Frances said. "I read about three or four books a week, mainly in the middle of the night when sleep forsakes me—but I love to read so it really doesn't matter what time it is."

Her diet and exercise regimens are basic yet impressive. Although she admits she can only eat whatever her teeth will allow her to, Frances says her rule is "eat, drink and be merry!" She did a lot of walking and regularly rode her Exercycle up until the age of 102! Now she suffers from some disintegrating vertebrae, which makes walking difficult—but she just uses a cane, or sometimes a wheelchair, to get where she wants to go.

Go she does, so you certainly couldn't call her sedentary—and you'll always find her dressed to the nines in a dress, hose, and heels, every day, whether she's got somewhere to go or not. She's celebrated her birthdays with "field trips," including a New York shopping spree for her 100th. A trip to London for 101 was planned, but she got sick just one week before so that trip had to be put on the shelf. But for 102 Frances was off to the races—horses, that is—in Kentucky, which she said was real fun even though she didn't win.

"I like to watch sports, and especially football on TV. I even had a friendly wager with my grandson on the Orange Bowl—and wisdom won over youth again, even if it is only just for fun!"

So Frances continues to have fun in life. She knows she's been blessed and is thankful for that, and she is still winning at this game we call life because she is driven—and no cops are in sight—to just keep doing everything right!

Barrett "Deemsy" Deems, 85

Chicago, Illinois

He's played with the best of the best—all the big names like Louis Armstrong, Benny Goodman, and the Dorsey Brothers. Today, he's still considered one of the greatest drummers of all time, and Deemsy may also just be one of the world's fastest drummers alive—at the amazing age of 85.

"Drumming keeps me young!" Deemsy proudly shared. "I play gigs four nights a week, have my own band and play with others, too. Everywhere I go, people can't believe I'm still playing—and frankly, I'm pretty amazed myself!"

When most people think about musicians playing in nightclubs and being involved in the music scene, the lifestyle is rarely considered healthy. But Deemsy prides himself on his clean living. Even though his work environment surrounded him with unhealthy temptations, he never drank, smoked, or took drugs because he got high from drumming. "I was always happy drumming—still am today, so I guess that's why I never needed other stimulants. I get high off what I do and drumming is definitely what I do!"

He doesn't miss a beat: if you were to hear him, you would never, ever believe he's 85. In fact, you'd think he was 25! Deemsy still jams with the best, and he is featured each night in at least two twenty-minute drum solos, where it's easy to see why he's still considered one of the world's fastest drummers ever. "I'll tell you what—it's a workout, that's for sure," Deemsy said. "Every part of my body is movin' and groovin'. In fact, the doctors have told me that my health is actually pretty darn good thanks to the exercise I get from drumming!"

Few people of any age can play the drums the way Deemsy does. As incredible as it is to still have the physical ability to play at the speed he does, it's equally amazing that the mind can think that fast to keep the body's reactions in step with such a ferocious pace.

"I may be getting older—but I haven't lost it—I've still got it and I can still play it! God's been good to me, but I've also helped him along the way by being good to me, too—so I guess we've got the right combination."

While Deemsy appreciates all that he's got and knows he's been blessed with a wonderful life, he will never let age dictate his life.

Kay Dennison, 77

Chula Vista, California

She's an advocate for seniors who says that her rewarding volunteer work is what really keeps her going—but she also admits it keeps her house a little messy! Kay is always on the go from one meeting to another, and although this dedication may have taken a toll on her personally, these experiences have also taught her a lot about life.

"I've always been interested in bettering the lives of others," Kay said, "whether it was helping my family or in my career as a nurse. Now I do it as a volunteer developing a grandparent support group for those who are raising their grandchildren and serving as full-time parents. This new trend is sweeping across our country, and there is virtually no road map to help. I'm trying to do something about that."

Kay's continual interaction with older adults enabled her to recognize that a number of grandparents were struggling with this issue, and they needed some support. "When it comes right down to it, many of them are dealing with grief over the loss of the ability to be a grandparent. Being thrown into the role of full-time parent is a very difficult transition. Our support group provides an outlet and an opportunity for them to share their thoughts with others who are experiencing the same thing. This way they see that they're not alone, and it gives them a chance to support each other."

Through Kay's continual giving and caring for others, she neglected herself somewhat and suffered a potentially life-threatening heart attack that has forced her to slow down. But she swears she'll only slow down physically, because mentally she's got too much learning still to do. "This health problem has taught me a lot. I've learned about patience and the value of meditation, yoga, and even water exercise. I've had to learn about grieving over my losses . . . like not being able to garden the way I used to. I've learned to grow in new ways—to do what I can and cuss what I can't!" she laughed. "I certainly don't mind my wrinkles and gray hair anymore—they're more like badges of honor now, and I'm proud to have earned them . . . that's my attitude!"

There is still little known about the role attitude plays in health and healing, but from what we do know, it may be that Kay subconsciously has had some influence. The doctors claim she stopped breathing three different times during her heart attack, and she believes them because she does remember being in a peaceful place where there was no pain.

Kay's experience has provided her with new understanding about life: you live with what you've got, appreciate what you have, and never, ever take life for granted. It's become the "Kay way" of life, and if everyone lived every day giving just half as much as she does, imagine how much better our world would really be.

Bhante Dharmawara, 108

Stockton, California

He is a humble Buddhist monk, yet he is also revered for his teachings and healing work. He's been referred to by the Dalai Lama as the "father of teachers" due to his ability to enlighten people on the purpose of life: to serve others. He is believed to be the oldest living monk in the world and considered by many to be a global treasure.

Bhante's spiritual path is undoubtedly key to his exceptionally long life. He is like a spiritual scientist, exploring what works for his heart, mind, and body by practicing and preaching one simple mantra: "You are what you think, eat, and drink." His life revolves around this belief, and for Bhante it has contributed to 108 years of living.

Bhante has not been a monk all his life; in fact, he led a very different life before studying Buddhism. Born in Phnom Penh, Cambodia, Bhante was trained in French schools and studied law and politics at the Sorbonne in Paris. During World War I he served as a recruiter for the French Army, enlisting Cambodian volunteers for the Allied cause. Later he became a distinguished magistrate and advisor in the king's court in Cambodia, where he served as a judge and administrator.

"Bhante lived 'the good life,' a life full of rich foods, smoking, drinking, and basically living it up," said Greg Lynn. "And Bhante says he did this until he 'used up' his vital life-force energy and became deathly ill."

Bhante felt unfulfilled despite his royal status, wealth and family. His search for inner peace, happiness, and the true meaning of life eventually led him to the forests of Thailand to study Buddhism, where he was taught by

a number of the most renowned Buddhist teachers in
the world. Through this experience he learned one very
important teaching: that "he, himself" was both the
problem and the solution. It was like a spiritual awakening that began a whole new life for Bhante and one he
continues to teach about today, seventy years later.

After spending several years in the forests, Bhante became a monk and reentered the world renewed and
committed to continuing his studies in India. He trained
in homeopathy and language, eventually learning how
to speak at least a dozen dialects fluently. In New Delhi,
Bhante founded the Asoka Mission, which grew to include a monastery, temple, meditation center, school,
and a health-care home, all run on his healing principles.
Today the Asoka Mission is still well known throughout
the world as one of the first spiritual centers to have a
youth hostel.

Bhante became globally recognized for his abilities.
He was elected president of the World Fellowship of
Buddhists and taught in the department of Asian lan-
guages at the Hindu university. During World War II, he
traveled on India's behalf to several countries, including
Japan, Germany, the United States, Britain, and the Soviet
Union, in an effort to seek a peaceful end to the war.

"During this time in India Bhante was very close
friends with Prime Minister Nehru, sharing a love of the
French language," Greg Lynn said. "Together, they were
friends with Mahatma Gandhi, and Bhante still brightens
when Gandhi's name is mentioned, saying he was 'quite a
witty fellow.' He fondly remembers Gandhi saying 'If one
is not his own physician by the age of 40, he is a fool!'"

The foundation of Bhante's healing and meditation
work today continues to revolve around what he considers to be the three most important elements: "I am what

I think, I am what I eat and I am what I drink! If we choose toxic food and toxic thoughts, we will feel the negative effects," Greg Lynn said. "Conversely, if we eat good foods and think good thoughts, then we feel good—Bhante believes it's just that simple."

The simplicity of this philosophy is its most enlightening attribute. "Affirmations are another example of the power of thought which help us become more conscious of how we choose to think, speak, and act. Then we become more aware of the effect each one has on us as individuals and on the world around us. Through this personal insight, we come to see more clearly that we are the creators of our own destinies and the destiny of the planet. It is like a form of prayer."

Aging affects all living species as a natural process of life. However, recognizing that thoughts create our words, which then create our actions, Bhante believes it's essential to maintain a positive outlook on one's daily existence. "A daily affirmation Bhante loves to share with others is 'May all beings be well and happy . . . JAI HO!'" said Greg Lynn. "It's a message that is both ageless and timeless—and one which will always carry significance and meaning in our lives."

This story was made possible by Greg Lynn Weaver, who helped translate Bhante's message. Greg Lynn serves as Bhante's healing assistant during his East Coast trips and stays at the PeaceWeavers centers.

Ray Dunn, 82

Carlsbad, California

He claims he has one of the finest-looking garages in town, with intricate cabinets and shelves he made himself. He bowls every week, reads, works on the computer, and is actively involved in a number of community organizations. All of this, and would you believe Ray is legally blind?

"The way I see it," Ray said, "I have a vision problem I can't do anything about. But I'm still going to enjoy life to the best of my ability and encourage others with visual impairments to do the same!" Ray had never heard of macular degeneration until he was diagnosed with it. He remembers first noticing something wrong with his vision when he saw wavy vertical lines out of one eye and figured he'd better see an ophthalmologist. "I was diagnosed with it in my left eye first and was told that I could have had it for quite awhile without even knowing it because the vision in my right eye was apparently good enough to compensate for the loss in my left."

It took two years before Ray's vision deteriorated to the point where he was designated legally blind. During that time he had laser treatments that helped slow down the progression but couldn't stop it completely. He still has some peripheral vision, so he's not completely blind, but he is blind enough to make driving impossible, and other tasks are a bit more challenging, too.

"I'm in the state of feel and fumbleness!" Ray said. "I feel around and fumble a bit—but I get the job done. I was landscaping and installing cabinets at our new home when my vision really went bad. It certainly made the tasks interesting, but I still figured out a way to work with my table saw and get it all done. Of course, my wife didn't think I could do it at first, so I'd just wait until she was gone and do it anyway. But she'll be the first to admit I really did a nice job!"

You have to be innovative when visually challenged. There are a variety of resources and tools available which make everyday tasks routine even for those who are blind, such as "talking books" on audiocassettes, closed-circuit TVs as reading machines, and computers that enlarge type to a legible size. New technology continues to be created every day to aid those who are visually challenged. "It's frustrating to hear that so few ophthalmologists are aware of the array of invaluable community services available to people, like the local Centers for the Blind. These groups are fabulous for folks to learn how to adjust to their changes and develop the necessary skills to continue living independently and doing what they love."

Ray attended two twelve-week training programs that taught him how to adapt and maintain his normal level of function, from mobility and cooking courses (not how to cook, but how to get around in the kitchen without sight) to typing and handicrafts, including knitting, which Ray admits was the only class he ever flunked!

"It's a great program that really helps you adjust and teaches you the necessary skills to gain confidence to keep on living your life. People enjoy it so much that when it's time to turn the tassel to the other side and graduate, no one ever wants to leave! But they do and know they can always go back for brushup skills!"

One of Ray's favorite activities is bowling, a sport he enjoyed in his youth. It had been twenty years since he last bowled, and starting up again as a legally blind person was something he never dreamed he would do.

Today, Ray plays in a weekly league with sighted bowlers, and he encourages others who are legally blind and interested in bowling by assisting them with a league that is exclusively for the visually challenged.

"If you could just hear the laughter and joy in their voices when they hear those pins fall, it really is something special," Ray said. "To realize that they can still do things they thought they couldn't is really important, regardless of what it is."

So Ray will continue doing his thing because he's never been one to just give up; now it's a message he shares with others, too.

Frank Eckert, 80

Carlsbad, California

Competition and a love of the water have long been a part of Frank Eckert's life. Every morning for twenty-one years he would wake up and perform his daily swimming ritual. Yet, it was this very love for the water and competition which forever changed, but also saved, his life.

Four years ago at the age of 76, while preparing for the world bodysurfing championships, he told his wife of fifty-six years, Genevieve, that he was going to the beach for a swim. Little did she know that it was actually bodysurfing he was doing. She discovered it later that afternoon when Frank complained about a feeling of numbness in his legs. The next thing she knew, he was on the floor saying that his legs weren't working right, and then they were off to the hospital.

"On the way, I asked him if he could think of anything that had happened recently to cause this," said Genevieve. "He said that maybe it was the tumble he took with a wave earlier in the day while bodysurfing. 'Bodysurfing,' I screamed, 'what in the world were you doing that for?'"

As it turned out, it was indeed the tumble he took in the ocean that created his condition, and the seriousness of the injury soon became evident. "The first team of doctors told us the numbness was most likely a pinched nerve and that as we get older the impact of such injuries is often more debilitating," Genevieve said. "But it quickly got worse, so we decided to get a second opinion. And it's a good thing we did, because it was far more than just a pinched nerve—Frank had crushed three discs in his spinal cord which caused the numbness in his lower body."

Frank is now fondly referred to as the "Titanium Man" due to the four-inch titanium plate surgically screwed into his spine. He's still swimming—in the pool only, he's pretty well given up bodysurfing, at least for now.

"The doctor said my fitness level and being in good shape were the reasons I had such a smooth recovery," Frank said. "And my never-give-up attitude enabled me to continue my love for swimming and competing after the accident."

Frank is still competing in events even after all that. He admits he doesn't swim like he used to, but he still enjoys it and therefore continues. And to make it even more incredible, just last year he also had an aortic valve replaced in his heart. "Being fit before all this happened helped me realize just how important taking care of your body really is, regardless of age. Even though it's different now, I'm still able to get out there, which is good for my rehabilitation, too. In fact, the doctor encourages my gym workout with weights and says it has absolutely helped lessen the amount of deterioration. I've won all the medals I need, but I will still give it my best—I'm not a quitter at anything, and certainly not my own life."

With a renewed sense of meaning in his life, Frank competes in the Senior Olympics, does his daily exercise routine, and continues to keep things in the proper perspective. "Every morning when I wake up, I thank God for giving me another day of togetherness with my wife. We have two beautiful children and two equally beautiful grandchildren, and that really is the best medal I'll ever receive!"

Lynn Edwards, 74

Brevard, North Carolina

She thinks more people could do what she does if they tried, claiming she's more active in her seventies than she was at forty. Lynn's a triathlete and is recognized as the oldest woman in the world to have completed the Ironman Triathlon in Kona, Hawaii. She has set the course record twice in her age group, first at the age of 69 and again at the age of 70.

The Ironman triathlon begins with a 2.4-mile swim (in the rough ocean waters of the Hawaiian Islands) followed immediately by a 112-mile bike ride (through the lava fields of Kona), and then a 26.2-mile run completes the day of exercise. All this must be completed within seventeen hours to be considered a legitimate finisher.

"There were times when I didn't finish, like the first time I entered, at age 63," Lynn said. "But honestly, being there with the potential to finish, was just as important. People often ask me why I do what I do, and it's actually very simple: it's about challenging myself and feeling better . . . that's really how it all began. I don't consider myself an athlete, because I was never into sports. Rather, this was achieved by sheer determination, setting goals, experiencing new adventures—all in an effort to be healthier as I got older."

Lynn's 40th birthday was a critical turning point: it was a festive affair, but it left Lynn feeling depressed. Cards from friends and family made subtle jokes about getting old, and although she didn't feel any older, the experience made her start thinking about her age. She began to wonder if it would become a time of doom and gloom as the cards suggested (albeit in a funny, loving way).

"Birthdays do seem to be a time of reflection, particularly significant decade marks like 40, 50, 60, etc. Our culture hasn't painted a very positive picture of aging. You start thinking things will inevitably begin to get worse—being you're that much closer to the end, suddenly you start taking a serious look at your life."

Although her health was relatively good, she started feeling the effects of smoking two packs of cigarettes a day. The extra weight she was carrying made her back ache, and she knew that without changes, the future wouldn't be a happy time of activity and fulfillment.

"It was time for a change. So I decided to take charge of my health and my future. I wanted to do more with the second half of my life than I did in the first half. I wasn't trying to be younger; in fact, it was quite the opposite—I wanted to be healthy and active *regardless* of my age . . . and I knew I was the only one who could make that happen!" Lynn began phase two of her life with a swimming program that helped her lose weight, reshape her body, and enabled her to cut back on her smoking, too. Learning how to swim was challenging and by accomplishing it later in life, she realized new skills could be learned. Age wouldn't be a barrier.

She began to rethink her own aging process and discovered she really wasn't as old as she had first thought, which enabled her to look more objectively at future possibilities. Lynn continued to grow by learning new things. She went back to school for her teaching credential, finished the master's degree she had started some twenty years earlier, and then had an eighteen-year career as a teacher and administrator. Lynn also participated in two Fulbright programs in India, fulfilled a dream to travel, and volunteered regularly in her community, including teaching an exercise class for seniors.

"The main reason I could do all of this was because of my improved health and energy levels, which are affected by more than just what we do physically," Lynn said. "It's a total package that requires using the body, mind, and soul in order to be truly healthy and energized with life."

Committed to trying new and different things, Lynn even began running at the age of 55. "Why not? The first time I ran a mile, it was exhilarating. However, in those days it wasn't lady-like. Women weren't supposed to sweat and be strong, so I had to keep it a secret. I'd wait until late at night when the neighbors were asleep, and then I'd sprint around the block!" Lynn said.

Lynn entered her first marathon at age 56, and even though she only ran eight of the twenty-six miles, within a year's time she did complete one. In the nineteen years since, Lynn has competed in more than 200 road races, forty triathlons, thirty-one marathons, and two ultramarathons. Her accomplishments are simply incredible, and even more so considering Lynn was never an athlete. Taking up running at the age of 55 is unique, but taking it to the next level of endurance competition and triathlons is absolutely extraordinary. At the age of 69,

Lynn not only achieved her goal of finishing the Iron-man, but she set a course record for her age group!

"I remember all the thoughts running through my mind the night before the race. Here I was at 69, won-dering if I couldn't do it at 63, why did I think I could do it now? But again, if you don't put yourself out there to try it, you'll never know. I'm glad I did, because the result was better than I imagined."

Lynn believes people can do more than they think they can, and thinking they can't may limit them more than anything else. "I think it's critical for people to be-lieve that it doesn't matter how old you are; it's about feeling good and being healthy all the way through life. Most people probably think I'm nuts or that I'm trying to defy the aging process, but that's not it at all. I don't want to be young again—I want to be the best I can and feel great regardless of my age."

Current research confirms Lynn's philosophy. Scien-tists studying the long-term health benefits of exercise have proven it provides a healthier heart, lower blood pressure and sturdier bones for all ages.

"You don't have to do what I do, but you have to do something . . . because if you don't use it, you will lose it! I'm proof that you can learn to do anything at any time in your life if you have the guts to go out and do it. It's hard getting older, but it's even harder if you give up on yourself and what's possible."

Birthdays don't bother Lynn anymore. "With each one I celebrate now, I actually feels like I'm in the best shape of my life—and at age 74, I think that's a pretty good thing to be feeling!" Lynn said.

Paul C. Fisher, 84

Boulder City, Nevada

Although he's known for his extraordinary business success, Paul considers himself a philosopher first and a businessman second. His philosophy is based on the most fundamental and basic formula: good luck results from applying the laws of nature, while pursuing accuracy, truth, fairness, and always doing what is morally and ethically right. He calls it the "scientific technique," a magic formula which is the real secret to his success.

It was a magic formula of a different kind, however, that launched Paul's business into outer space—literally. He is the founder, owner, and president of the Fisher Space Pen Company, the creator and manufacturer of the revolutionary "Space Pen." Considered a scientific breakthrough, this state-of-the-art pen will write consistently in virtually any situation. It has been used on all manned spaceflights by NASA's astronauts since Apollo 7 in 1967, and by the Russian Cosmonauts as well. His pen has also been used by the Everest Ski Expedition, the Cousteau Society, the F.B.I., the U.S. Armed Forces, the London and Berlin police forces and the Kennedy and Houston Space Centers. Additionally it is displayed at the Museum of Modern Art in New York and the Smithsonian Air and Space Museums.

Paul is more than just a manufacturer of pens. He is an inventive engineer who continues to improve the ballpoint pen, a product he helped pioneer in 1945 as one of the original designers of the Reynolds Pens, the first ballpoint pens sold in America and most of the world. Since that time Paul has created a multimillion-dollar business with his variety of pen products. He's still inventing, creating, and perfecting his trade today as he prepares to launch the company's latest product: the Millennium-Mars Space Pen, guaranteed to write for an entire lifetime—or as Paul claims, "until man sets foot on Mars."

"We started our business fifty years ago and are still known for creating new and better products. We always strive to improve upon what we learned from our previous experiences, and that has been the key to our success," Paul said. "Again, it's the scientific technique . . . the only commonsense way to solve any problem, in any

field. To discover a truly correct answer, we must observe and think with absolute accuracy in observing and utilizing what our experiences can teach us. It's the same marvelous technique that helped men and women create television, jet planes, space travel, and computers."

Paul compares the human mind to a modern-day computer. "Our minds are programmed, in a sense, by our experiences. We're born with a basic type of hardware and software, but it's the experiences that program the facts and information into our minds, which we then use to seek out the answers to solve our problems. That's why humans have minds. We'll never solve any problem without absolute accuracy; yet it is still very difficult to achieve, particularly in the social sciences of economics, philosophy, religion, ethics, politics, etc. They are very complicated subject matters."

Striving for complete accuracy may seem unrealistic to some since humans are not perfect. Paul's belief and practice is to always strive for perfection and use experience as the guide—trial and error is how we learn to solve problems. In 1960 he applied his scientific technique theory to tax reform, inflation, and unemployment, and he published a book on the topic, *Road to Freedom*. To promote the book and his campaign for tax reform, he even entered the 1960 New Hampshire presidential primary and ran against John F. Kennedy and Richard M. Nixon. Paul received considerably more votes than any other losing Democratic candidate had ever received and won the respect of many people, including President Kennedy, who later asked Paul to help improve the pens used by the U.S. Post Office. Paul obliged by offering to rewrite the specifications, and even today governments throughout the world, including our state governments, are still using his original specifications.

Paul believes thought is one of the most powerful forces in the world and that there may be such a thing as mental telepathy; thoughts may actually control many things that happen in the physical world.

"It's a theory I cannot prove, but this philosophy has worked for me in many remarkable ways. When you believe and have a vision, you can make it happen . . . especially if the thoughts are right, and strong enough. Some of my best ideas have come to me in the middle of the night, which is one of the reasons I live above the business, because these visions and bursts of intuition seem to happen at night. I envisioned the company's first product, the chrome-plated Bullet Pen, one night in a dream."

Although he can't possibly explain this, or the powers of the human mind, he says he cannot explain God, either. He is inclined to believe in divine inspiration because he has experienced many personal psychic experiences. He says that since we live in a virtually limitless world that goes to infinity in all different directions, it's virtually impossible for the human mind to grasp and understand it all.

"Everything humans have experienced has a beginning and an end, but it's what lies beyond which is so intriguing. I'm not sure we'll ever be able to explain what we can't see—all our thoughts, how we derive them, and all the other intangibles in our world. They may always remain a mystery—one we may never, ever solve."

One problem Paul believes can be solved is how to increase human happiness and reduce human suffering. "Human happiness is sacred— the most important thing in the world—because life without happiness has no value. The key to happiness is self-respect and self-esteem. We should always do what is physically, morally, and ethically right, to the best of our abilities. If we think positively and have the vision of being in harmony with God and nature, good things will happen."

And good things continue to happen to Paul. His business has earned record profits, but more importantly, he is happy and continues to strive to help others achieve the same success and happiness. "Being a good inventor means keeping your mind open, focused, and accurate in order to learn what experience can teach you. If people who are failing in any aspect of their lives can just train themselves to do this—be more accurate and truthful—they may turn their lives around and become happier and more successful, too. It all goes back to the fundamentals of inventing. Inventors don't really create; they discover by trial and error, through experience of what works and what doesn't. We need minds that are trained to be objective and accurate if we are to learn correctly what experience can teach us. We must always be open-minded and willing to learn."

Since experience is key, one of the most fabulous aspects of growing older is the accumulation of experiences that results in real wisdom . . . perhaps the ultimate secret formula.

Florence Foster, 94

Jackson, Michigan

Florence feels that fun and faith are the foundations for her longevity, and at age 94 she also recognizes that being blessed with good health has played a part, too. But the real secret to her aging success may be her spunky, get-up-and-go outlook on life. "I have fun all the time—age has nothing to do with that!" she said. Not only is she having fun in her own life, she's helping others have fun too.

Florence figured it was time for a change in the design of the ugly gray metal canes used by people in her age group. Her drive for fun and ingenuity launched a fabulous new spin on the old-fashioned cane, changing the product's tired image into one exemplifying creativity, uniqueness, and definite personality.

"I was headed for Arizona to hike with my daughter and knew it would be helpful if I had a little support, like a cane, for the unlevel surfaces of the terrain. But my only choice was the standard hospital rental, and that just wouldn't do it for me—those were for old people!" Florence said. "If I used one of those, people would've started treating me as if I was old . . . and then I might believe them!"

Florence set out to find a way to add a little color and fun to the old cane concept. She found herself at a local auto-parts factory asking for a clear plastic tube about one inch in diameter that could be filled with different things and have a handle and rubber tip applied at the ends. It was "do-able," she was told, and the next thing she knew, presto—Florence became an entrepreneur! The Florence Foster Cane is currently being produced by the Plastigage Corporation, so now others can experience the fun and freedom it provides, too.

"The first one I made for myself was filled with a string of colorful mini silk roses, and when I took it to Arizona, I could barely leave the house without someone asking me about my walking stick. I know there are a lot of people like me who could use the support of a cane to get around better and more often but would never use one of those other ones. But there weren't any other options," Florence said. "The cane's image may not be good, but the concept is great . . . it just needed a little updating and some creativity. Now, maybe those who've never used one will give it a try, have some fun and even get out and do more without the risk and fear of falling."

Since starting this venture Florence has received letters from people all over the country who are thoroughly enjoying her product and their new lifestyle. "It's not about making money—it's the great stories people send telling me of their newfound freedom and even friendships that have developed since they've used their new canes. One of my favorites was from a granddaughter who bought one for her grandmother's 100th birthday! She had not been very active, but ever since she got her birthday cane she's gone nonstop, showing it off to all her friends and even made new friends in the process."

Florence firmly believes that faith has played a significant role in her life and that God had this very plan in mind for her to "give other older adults some fun . . . to get 'em out and get 'em going again," and her Foster Cane is now enabling that to happen.

"Life is meant to be celebrated . . . that's the way I see it," Florence said. "Every morning I read a Bible verse I have taped to my mirror: 'This is the day the Lord has made. Rejoice and be glad in it!' That is how I start and live every day of my life. You just can't have a bad day after that—rejoicing makes it a good day!"

With the personal motto "If it's meant to be, it's up to me!" Florence is determined to help others and herself have fun in life. She will continue her daily exercises to keep her good health, stay involved with photography, church, family, and friends and continue to live a "balanced" life with a good attitude—so she can stay alive and have fun a little while longer.

Rose Freedman, 104

Beverly Hills, California

Rose couldn't be happier—the Los Angeles Lakers basketball team is off to their best start ever, 11-0! "It's the best start in the history of the franchise," said Rose, who may know more about the Lakers than most fans half her age.

Rose is indeed a sports fan—but she's an absolute Lakers fanatic! And she just may have something to do with this season's great start since she was sitting with Lakers owner, Jerry Buss, on opening night. "They call me their 'Lucky Charm.' I'm definitely one of their biggest fans . . . and probably one of the oldest, too. That's what keeps me young, staying involved with all the things I love!"

Being a sports fan has come full circle for Rose. She raised three children, including two boys, and doubts there are many mothers with sons who don't get hooked on sports. Today her entire family, including the grand-kids, is into sports—especially Laker basketball—and matriarch Rose leads the way.

"To say she goes through withdrawal during the off-season is an under-statement," said Rose's daughter, Arlene. "The whole family is always happy to see the basketball season begin . . . at least we know where Mom will be—watching her beloved Lakers!"

Evidently the Lakers are equally proud to have a fan like Rose. In honor of her 100th birthday, they paid a spe-cial tribute to her at half-time with a plaque naming Rose the Lakers number one fan. She also got a happy birthday serenade from the entire team, band, and enthusiastic crowd. "I was out there in the middle of the court cele-brating my 100th birthday with the Lakers! Jerry West gave me a Lakers jersey with my name in letters on the back, and number 100 to boot! Plus, A. C. Green, Byron Scott, and James Worthy were with me too . . . it was un-believable and unforgettable!"

Her love for the Lakers is genuine and is apparently reciprocated. Whenever she sees any of the players around town, she is always amazed when they remem-ber her and stop to visit. "After Magic left, I told James

Worthy he was my favorite, so now he always seems to remember me!" Of course, it's easy to see why Rose is so easy to remember. She has a great outlook on life and is in good health except for being a little hard of hearing. She takes no pills, loves to shop, thrives on learning, and believes family is always number one. "My family's the most important thing in my life and they're what really keep me going. They treat me nice and are always watching over, so I feel truly blessed to have such a loving and caring family."

Rose also takes good care of herself. She lives on her own, exercises daily, and loves to cook, but has recently started enjoying a new special treat—having lunch out. "After cooking all these years, even though I love it, it's a nice change of pace to go out for lunch. Maybe I should have done this sooner since I'm having so much fun, but I guess it's better late than never!"

One thing Rose is rarely late for and certainly never misses is a sale! In fact, she readily admits one of her favorite pastimes is shopping. Rose says you're never too old for a bargain, especially a 15-percent discount on your birthday! In fact, she loves shopping so much that the running family joke is if they can't find her and it's not Laker season, they have her paged at Loehmann's department store! "She's undoubtedly one of the most elegant women I know," Arlene said. "And she dresses to the nines . . . the phrase 'California casual' never made its way to her wardrobe. Of course, that's because she was a careerwoman in New York and always dressed to the hilt, so she knows no different. She's never worn a pair of sweats or jeans in her life and probably never will. Dressing casual to her means a skirt and blouse, with heels and nylons too!"

In fact, on one of her latest trips to Mexico she walked the town's cobblestone streets in heels! Sneakers, though offered and undoubtedly more comfortable, were completely unacceptable to her. She considered them an appalling accessory to her attire—a fashion statement she was not about to make.

The trip to Mexico was planned to fulfill her continual love of learning, Spanish specifically, because languages are her passion. "My daughter took me to San Miguel de Allende, a famous artist's colony four hours north of Mexico City, which has an institute where foreigners go to learn Spanish. We went to school every day and lived right there in their community in order to experience the culture in a unique and meaningful way. I speak six different languages and can even read and write many of them too . . . I just love to learn, always have and expect I always will."

Rose believes you're never too old to learn new things and that learning keeps you young. As a result, she says she never feels old. "I learned about baseball this year, too, by going to my first professional ballgame . . . how about that, seeing your first Dodgers game at 104!" But if the Dodgers are looking for a good-luck charm—they'd better look again, because Rose has already been spoken for by another professional sports team in town.

Audrey George, 73

Escondido, California

No time for naps. No time to be sick. No time to be bored. And no time to be around people who mope and whine about nothing to do when there's so much doing that needs to be done. Audrey says she's busier now that she's retired than when she worked full-time, because giving is living, and this is how Audrey lives her life.

"It's real satisfying to help others," Audrey said. "And there's such a variety of things to get involved with. I just can't understand how anyone can complain about being bored, because it really is a choice one makes on their own. Volunteering is a terrific way to be involved with life, and I've also created my own little family of friends in the process."

After retiring from a career in dentistry, Audrey instinctively knew that she wanted to be involved in something new, because she believed that when you stop learning you stop living—so off to school she went. But she didn't go to a typical university or community college. Audrey went to OASIS (Older Adult Service and Information Services) and took a variety of classes ranging from computers and religion to health, psychology, and art. She also helped in the office and with class registration, but then Audrey went back to real school to help children learn, too.

"OASIS sponsors an intergenerational tutoring program where older adults serve as special tutors to elementary-age students and some older students too," Audrey said. "We help them with their reading—how to better understand and enjoy what they read so they'll look forward to reading rather than just doing it because they have to."

The volunteers don't need teaching experience, just a love of children and a desire to help them learn. A six-week training program, taught by teachers, provides volunteers with an overview of the appropriate strategies and techniques needed to tutor children.

"This is a much-needed program today because even though the kids are really wonderful, some need a little extra attention. This one-on-one opportunity provides a regular relationship with someone who is there just for them, which gives us a strong foundation to build on in order to help. We work with the child throughout the course of the entire school year, and that consistency is key to the results we achieve together."

Audrey started tutoring with just one child one day a week and has now expanded to working with three children two days a week. She says it's among the most fulfilling work she's ever done. She looks forward to her time with each little friend and knows that this is something she will do to the end. "I'll always make time to help children, because it really does make a difference in their lives. Giving of my time is such a small price to pay to provide something so meaningful to someone else which will last their entire lives."

With all the time Audrey spends doing for others, it's hard to believe she has much time to take care of herself. Perhaps giving helps, because she's in excellent health. "I don't have any time to be sick, so I make sure I eat right, get the proper amount of exercise, and rest—when it's time for bed, I'm out like a light!" she laughed. "And when my body clock wakes me up at 6:30 A.M., I'm ready to begin again!"

Audrey starts each day with a two- to three-mile walk with her dog, Josh, and usually walks a mile in the late afternoon, too. She also loves to cook and regularly entertains friends with her healthy dining creations. Audrey's routine keeps her energized, happy and able to continue doing for others—which she says has nothing to do with age. "I like to give of myself to help someone else. And I don't think anyone is ever too old to do that. Besides, you're as old as you feel. I'm always charged up and feeling great because giving gives me the zest for life and living."

LeRoy "Granny" Grannis, 80

Carlsbad , California

His nickname may conjure up an unlikely image for a surfing legend, but then again you have to consider the source: younger surfers who consider anyone over the age of 50 old, let alone someone who is 80 and still hitting the waves on a daily basis.

So "Granny" seems to fit LeRoy, a man who never lets age get in his way. He works around it and claims if you hang around long enough, you automatically become a "legend" at anything you do . . . strictly by default! "I started surfing at the age of 14 in Hermosa Beach, and I simply see no reason to stop doing something you really enjoy because of age. Now, I don't surf like I used to by any means, but I really enjoy getting out in the surf every day . . . even if I'm just hanging out, paddling around."

You may remember Granny from a Nike television commercial featuring him and three of his surfing buddies from the 1930s. Granny has done several interviews for TV shows, magazines, and newspapers over the years. Apparently the notion of surfing being considered exclusively as a sport for the young is now starting to change.

"Hey, I got into something that I really love and my body still allows me to go out there and do it . . . so I do!" Granny said. And Granny's love for surfing opened up career opportunities for him as well. He was instrumental in helping start *Surfing* magazine, and was also a staff photographer for both *The Reef* and *Surfer* magazines in the 1960s. "It was great . . . if I wasn't riding the waves, I was shooting them, and I still go out and regularly photograph the sport today."

In addition to taking surfing photographs, Granny was also a staff photographer for *Hang Gliding* magazine and traveled annually to Telluride, Colorado to shoot the Hang Glider Free-Falling Festival. "Air photography is just incredible there, truly magnificent," Granny said. "I flew tandem . . . let someone else do the driving so I could concentrate on taking the pictures. And it's something I continued doing until just a few years ago."

Granny has been blessed with good health, except for a nagging inner-ear problem that kept him out of the water for more than a year. "I figured I had to do something—just sitting on my board in the water, would be better than nothing," Granny remembered. "So I just started paddling around, graduated to my knees, and actually ended up riding bigger waves from my knees than I probably ever would have standing!"

Being out in the waves feels good to Granny, and it's more than just physical—the companionship and camaraderie are equally important. "Talking surf with the guys and being together is great stuff. Plus, I know everybody . . . and it seems lots of them know me too, so if I love being out there and they love seeing me out there . . . it's a good thing all around, I guess."

His kids seem happy their "old man" still surfs, and it's perhaps a tribute to the sport's staying power and healthful benefits that an 80-year-old body can still go out and do it.

"I think too many people think older people can't do anything," Granny said. "And even some of the older people themselves believe that when you get to a certain age, you better slow down. Well, that's just not my style . . . I don't believe you should ever let age stop you from doing anything . . . ever!"

Cecily Green, 69

Oceanside, California

E very day is a celebration of life for Cecily. She believes that she's been blessed with twenty-five "bonus years" and counting, after being diagnosed with breast cancer in her early forties and given a prognosis of little chance of survival.

"Cancer ran rampant through my family history, including breast cancer," Cecily said. "But I guess it's one of those things you just don't think about and certainly never think will happen to you . . . but it did. I was showering one morning, felt a small lump and had it checked that very day. Three days later I was in the hospital having a Halsted radical mastectomy to remove the cancer."

The following months and years were a time for healing. Initially it began with intensive radiation therapy followed by continued physical healing. Emotional healing, unmeasured in scientific and medical realms, is also an essential element for survival. "When you're facing death, you reevaluate your life to help prepare yourself, your family, and those around you for what may happen. The months following the surgery were traumatic, not necessarily just for me, but for my family. Then I suffered the death of my mother, which sent me into a total tailspin."

For the first time in her life, Cecily became her own priority. This process not only gave her strength, but those around her became stronger too. "Two years after my diagnosis, during my recovery period, I went back to school and began a whole new life," Cecily said. "I became a counselor and helped others who were critically ill better understand their condition and work positively toward either healing or accepting it, depending on their individual situation. I didn't know how long I had to live, so I absolutely made the best of every day . . . and still do. I felt that if I could help others with this process, that would be a great thing for me, and hopefully for them, too. I often think that this all happened to me for a reason, because I've had the opportunity to share my story to help others."

Cecily recently celebrated the twenty-fifth anniversary of surviving breast cancer and really "whooped it up!" Since breast cancer often carries a twenty-year waiting period before one can be considered really out of the woods, she says she now joyously heaves a deep sigh of relief every day and has no plan to change this routine anytime soon.

"I've learned so much through this—about me, life, just everything! I am a survivor. I even overcame thyroid and cervical cancer in between all this. What I think I learned most though, was to pay attention to signs along the way. Don't be so busy and wrapped up in being on the go all the time that you ignore warning signs in your body—pay attention and don't wait for the sky to fall on you to make you see it!"

Every day Cecily makes a statement about cancer and survival. She has intentionally chosen not to wear a prosthesis so people can see that it's O.K. to have cancer, to survive it, and to continue participating in all aspects of life. Her contribution is to help people accept cancer as a part of life rather than feeling ashamed about it, which Cecily believes is more common than people think.

"I've become more aware of this not only through my own process, but really through my counseling work with others. It's as much a priority to help people heal emotionally as well as physically from cancer and other critical-illness diagnoses. I do believe this has definitely become more of a priority among the medical profession, too. The healing of the whole person is finally getting attention. Hope and love can help heal too."

Of course, Cecily had her own unique healing strategies, which even included attending a nudist camp. It helped her overcome one of her biggest fears: adjusting and accepting the physical changes the cancer created. If not for the cancer, she doubts she would have ever gone.

She's committed to helping others, too, and encourages people to take control over their lives, which Cecily believes is key to being able to celebrate life, at any age. "Life's so precious . . . when you realize that, age just doesn't matter—it's about living and celebrating the fact that you are alive," Cecily said. "I guess I really don't get too caught up in the age thing, because to me, every day is a victory since I never really expected to be here to see it. As a result, I'm incredibly proud of my age and feel sorry for those who don't share that same enthusiasm about life. Age should be looked at as a badge of honor, a reward for succeeding at life's challenges!"

Bennie Harden, 105

Ramona, California

S taying alive 'til 105 means you are doing something right. And "right" is the word Bennie uses to
describe her extraordinary life. "I just lived my life
right, treated everybody right, ate right, and always
tried to do the right thing," Bennie shared. "We always
went to Sunday school, did our chores, I never smoked
or drank, and I don't buy all those packaged things at
the grocery store . . . I've always liked the fresh stuff."

Raised on a farm, Bennie learned early in life about
the importance of eating right. She said that most everything she ate was fresh and likely grown on their land. "I
can remember always having fresh vegetables on the
table, and all the dairy products came from our own
cows and the eggs from our chickens. And I don't ever
remember not having honey on the table—fresh, sweet,
and there's just nothing better than that . . . except maybe
turnips and hot cornbread! It may sound weird to some
people, but they obviously don't know how to make it,
because those are two of my favorite foods ever! And for
my birthday, among all the candy, cake, cookies, and
pies, I still liked my gift of black-eyed peas best!"

Bennie believes in the simple joys of life, like family
and friends and being blessed with good health. In all
her days she's only been to the hospital once, and that
was for cataract surgery. She still lives on her own with
her daughter close by, is as feisty as ever, and her spirit's
strong—undoubtedly a tribute to having lived so long.
"I have no idea what the secret is, but everyone I meet
tells me I'm the oldest person they've ever met," Bennie

said. "I can't believe that I'm such a big deal . . . but it's fun just the same, because I've got stories to tell."

Born in 1893, Bennie has already lived in two centuries and is pushing for a third. She's seen the creation of countless inventions, including the automobile. Most every modern convenience taken for granted today, did not exist when Bennie was young. "Children are fascinated with the stories I tell. They gather 'round to hear the tales of my days and are simply amazed at all that has changed. They can't imagine living without indoor plumbing and the abundance of other conveniences. Times have changed, and as a result we may be facing a time when people have just simply too much stuff."

One thing that Bennie believes there will never be enough of is the love of a family. She's proud of her group as it grows bigger each year—she's up to six generations now, and it's always a house full of cheer. And cheer they all did at Bennie's 105th birthday bash, which they are quite certain won't be her last.

Rosie Harris, 77

Los Angeles, California

Rosie loves to learn, and after growing up without the opportunity for much schooling, she is happy to report that time and age have worked in her favor—she now holds both high school and college degrees. "I had to drop out of school in the tenth grade," said Rosie. "But I was determined to get my diploma, no matter how old I was when I did it. As it turned out, I graduated from high school along with my children, so it was indeed a very special time in my life."

Rosie's desire to learn didn't stop after she received her high school diploma. She had college and career ideas to pursue, and the new field of gerontology absolutely fascinated her. Rosie went to college on a part-time basis and received her degree in gerontology at age 63.

"I marched so proudly in that graduation ceremony. Who would have thought that I would have been doing that at my age? But I guess it just goes to show, you're never too old!"

Shortly after graduation, she moved to California where it was warm and closer to one of her daughters. The job search was as difficult for Rosie, as it is for many new graduates. She had nearly given up the idea of working in gerontology when she heard about the Andrus Volunteer program at the University of Southern California Gerontology Center."

"I signed up for the new-member orientation meeting and never left," she said. "I help provide information at the front desk and work with a team of volunteers who visit local schools and teach children about aging and ageism. Plus I attend our regular meetings and even take classes at the university, too."

In addition to her Andrus volunteer work, Rosie does missionary work for her church and plans to talk with the church school about starting a flower garden to help kids learn the importance of growing and all that comes with it. "Doing for others is good for the soul, and it's sure nice to wake up in the morning knowing you have something to look forward to doing—and even better when you know there's someone looking forward to having you be there to do it," Rosie explained. "Feeling useful and contributing in life is important at all ages. It's all about learning, growing, and giving. If more people would learn to give—especially of themselves, as they grow older—I think there would be a lot of good in that for everyone."

Sam Hartman, 82

North Hollywood, California

"You can't teach an old dog new tricks" is a saying many apply to people, but learning is lifelong, and if you stop, that may be when you start to get old. Sam believes you're never too old to learn, and he prides himself on all the new things he's learned in his later years. He is a wizard on the computer—he learned an elaborate stargazing program and another for recording his family tree. But he never would have imagined that his interest in computers would lead him into the literary world. Now he even describes himself as totally "hooked" on writing.

"A friend told me about this weekly writing workshop that meets at our local senior center," Sam recalled. "I kept putting it off because I'm really not the group 'joiner' type, until one day when I ran out of excuses and decided to go along. To my complete surprise, I really enjoyed it—the mental stimulation was fun and challenging—so I stuck with it, and now I'm completely hooked! I'm not an accomplished writer, but I have written about sixty-five stories, articles, and poems to date!"

Sam recognizes that discovering new interests seems only to occur when you are open and receptive enough to put yourself in places where you can try different things. If you expose yourself to enough experiences, there's bound to be one that really clicks. Too often, particularly as people get older, they think they know everything about themselves and figure that if something was of real interest to them, they would have pursued it already. "I never thought I'd have an interest in writing, let alone an ability, because I spent my entire career as a heavy-equipment mechanic—that's about as far away from writing as you can get," Sam said. "But at this point in my life, with the variety of changes taking place, including the death of my wife, writing has been a healthy outlet to help with my loneliness, release some of my emotions, and express my true feelings."

The writing group of ten men and women has also become a social outlet for Sam. Most are in their eighties and discovered their love for writing later in life also. They share a meaningful camaraderie while expanding their minds, and they all genuinely like each other while sharing a joy of writing.

"It's so easy to go into a shell as you get older," Sam said. "Especially when you lose a spouse, your best friend, or loved one . . . you kind of forget how to make friends or how to interact with others, so people just tend to avoid it all together. But it's really important to

115

stay connected with people and activities—otherwise it seems like you're just waiting to die, and that's not how I want to spend my time here!"

Sam's had his share of health battles; he's already lost one lung and is currently operating on what he calls "one cylinder." He's been diagnosed with emphysema, so at this point his attitude about life is to do the best he can with what he has to work with. His mental powers are as sharp as a tack, so he still continues to challenge and stimulate his mind.

"Age can't be the excuse to not make the effort to try new things—we've all been brainwashed to think people can't continue growing and learning as we get older," Sam said. "I actually think this is the time in life to do new things because we finally have the time to explore new horizons. It's amazing what you can still learn about yourself that you never, ever knew."

Sam's convinced that aging is a state of mind and wishes more people would recognize that life is about learning, experimenting, and trying new things. He agonizes over friends he knows who simply spend their days watching the cars go by and the grass grow. It's a tragic waste, and he feels sorry for them because there's so much more to life.

"My newfound love for writing has made me realize things about myself that I never would have otherwise—like how I don't want to grow old with no one to talk to, write to, or care for. I like having people around to share and learn with, because to me, that's what makes life worth living."

Eugene, 87, and Wilda, 93, Haskell

San Diego , California

Theirs is a true love story, love not just for each other, but for music and children, too. After seventy years of living separate lives, they reunited after a high school reunion and picked up right where they left off: in love. They married shortly thereafter, the beautiful bride age 93 and the handsome groom 87. Their love of music is how their story began, and their desire to make a difference in children's lives with music is how their story will end.

"Having a passion keeps you alive," Gene shared. "Both Wilda and I have been passionate about music all our lives. And we were also passionate about each other when we were younger—we just had to wait seventy years to put it all together."

Wilda was Gene's high-school music teacher, fresh from the University of Southern California (USC), when the two first met. He was 16 and she was 22, but it was love at first sight, and music was at the center of their love. A senior at the time, Gene won a scholarship to USC, and the two then became a couple. During his sophomore year Gene asked Wilda to be his bride. Although she accepted, unfortunately, Gene's parents didn't think it was time for him to be marrying, so they stepped in and forbade the marriage. Heartbroken, Gene left for Stanford University for his final two years, during which time his contact with Wilda became less frequent, and the two drifted apart.

They each went on with their lives, sharing their love of music—just independently. Wilda taught music for thirty-five years in the classroom where she and Gene met, and eventually married and adopted a daughter. Gene earned both a bachelor's and master's degrees and became the superintendent of schools for Santa Cruz before eventually earning a doctorate and writing his dissertation about the use of music in the classroom to motivate learning and build character in children.

"When I finished my dissertation I had a choice to make," Gene remembered. "I was offered a position as the superintendent for the Los Angeles city schools, or I could go to Harlem, New York, and prove my theory by getting the opportunity to work with music and children. I agonized about the decision for a week, but I kept coming back to thoughts of Wilda and the difference music made in my life."

So off he went to one of the most challenging schools in the country to prove his theory. As it turned out, he took his theory far beyond just the classroom. "I remember meeting with the principal of the school, and after he saw my credentials he couldn't believe I wanted to be there," Gene said. "It was in a gang-infested area, the classroom had become a dumping ground for students other teachers couldn't control, and in fact, the kids had run the previous three teachers out, including locking one in the closet. This was the exact type of challenge I wanted, because I believed in my theory and I was ready to prove it."

There were bars on the windows, teachers used whistles to get the students' attention, and the place was being run more like an institution than a classroom. Gene had never seen a more hostile, unhappy group of children in his life, and deep down he knew it could only get better. And it did. At the same time that the students were sizing him up, figuring out which stunt they would pull next, Gene said he looked up toward the heavens and asked God what he should do. The next thing he knew he was addressing the group, saying he'd heard there were some great singers among them, and that was the beginning of the musical magic.

"A young black girl stood up, said she could sing and began to perform the most angelic rendition of one of the greatest spiritual tunes, 'He's Got the Whole World In His Hands,'" Gene said. "At the end, it was so quiet you could hear a pin drop. Then suddenly, the other kids began raising their hands, saying 'Teach, we can sing too, I've got a song, I've got a song!' It was really beautiful, and at that very moment I knew I'd made the right decision."

Gene continued to challenge and encourage them with music and goal-setting. He helped them believe in themselves, and with that belief they could accomplish anything they set their minds to. Their first goal as a class was to perform a show, a big Broadway-type musical production. Together they made it happen. The girls went to businesses in the area to get donations for fabric to make their costumes, and the boys collected refrigerator boxes for cardboard to build the set. At the end of the year, together they performed *Hansel and Gretel*.

The superintendent of the New York city schools attended their final performance, and was so impressed that he invited Gene to the Board of Education meeting to explain what he had done. He hoped to make it a model program for the entire school district.

"I believed my theory could work all over the country, and so at that very moment I asked the superintendent to be the chairman of the board of Lyric Theatre International, an organization for high schoolers based on the principles of my dissertation." It worked, and music was once again making a difference in children's lives. Gene spent the next ten years developing the Harlem program before moving back home to Los Angeles at the request of Mayor Tom Bradley, who wanted Gene to bring his musical magic to Watts. "Being back in Los Angeles made me think about Wilda even more," Gene said. "And I couldn't help but feel that my success was also hers, because this was a dream we had shared together long ago, to help children believe they can change themselves, their image, who they are and who they can be, through music and having a goal."

Gene created the Royal Champions of the World for his Los Angeles contingency, a group sponsored by Lyric Theatre International. He challenged the youths from Watts to treat themselves like royalty, erase racism, refuse to pollute their bodies with drugs, and promote peace through their voices. He asked them where was the most incredible place they could think of to perform, giving them a goal to strive for. The unanimous answer: at the White House for President Ford.

"Initially, I don't think the kids really believed they could do this," Gene admitted. "But that was part of the teaching, to help them understand what it takes to achieve a goal . . . attitude, gratitude, and a belief in themselves as winners. And once they learned this, we did make it to the White House!"

Over the years Gene's programs (with Wilda's spirit always with him) reached more than three million people around the world, including four-thousand performances throughout the United States, as well as in China, Japan, New Zealand, and Europe. The groups have performed for world leaders such as Pope John Paul II, President Ford, and the Shah and Empress of Iran. They also received an unprecedented invitation to perform at the United Nations.

"The real success of the story is how this changed the lives of so many at-risk children," Gene said, "kids who might otherwise be in gangs or who might never know what they're capable of. Music is transforming. It can change your life, just as it did mine, and I've been able to help others experience how it can change theirs. When you're passionate about something, it really does make life worth living."

Although Gene was passionate about his work, his love life never seemed to recover from the loss of Wilda, even after all those years. He married twice and divorced twice, and while he did have a beautiful daughter from his first marriage, he remained forever hopeful that true love would again someday come his way.

While planning a reunion with his high-school classmates to mark the sixty-sixth anniversary of graduation, Gene learned that his former music teacher, Wilda, was still in town. Although she was unable to attend the affair, Wilda was interested in seeing Gene again, so they decided to schedule a meeting a few weeks later at a special historical place (just like them): the Hotel del Coronado in San Diego, California.

"When she opened the door it was like time stood still. We looked into each other's eyes and everything was exactly the same, even after all these years. Love never leaves, and we are a tribute to that. We picked up right where we left off, and together again we are making our dream come true to enlighten children's lives through music and finally sharing our lives as one."

It's amazing what you can achieve, if only you believe. Both Gene and Wilda certainly believe, and it's evident that for them the best is yet to be. Bravo!!

Bill Henderson, 99

Oceanside, California

H e never expected to live this long. In fact, he's even outlived his life insurance—paid off at the age of 85—and his funeral insurance, too! When filing his last income taxes, the computer software didn't even recognize his birthdate because it was in the last century: 1898, to be exact. As far as the future goes, he says he never plans too far ahead . . . except maybe for the design of a new woodcarving, which may be part of the secret of his success.

A carpenter by trade, Bill fondly remembers carving wooden boats as a boy in Vermont. This artistic penchant for carving has endured, and some of his finest work and most prized pieces were created in his later years. "I enjoy it immensely," Bill said. "It gives me an outlet, it's something I can do with others or alone, and it's a way for me to express myself artistically. I've made a lot of friends through carving, and it's something that still has special meaning to me."

Bill has been carving artistic pieces for more than twenty-five years and says each becomes a special work in itself. Sometimes he has a specific plan in mind and other times he is simply inspired by the wood itself, its shape, color, and overall features.

"I remember finding an intriguing piece of twisted root while out on a walk one day . . . I knew it was special but just didn't know exactly why at the time," Bill said. "I even walked a half-mile back to my car just to get a saw to cut it . . . and that root has become one of my most favorite works ever."

It was several years before Bill, then in his eighties, determined that there was a lady in that twisted piece of root. The intricate and impressive carving of a woman's delicate features—eyes, nose, mouth, and even the strands of her hair—as well as her hands and feet, are truly beautiful.

Bill says he doesn't pay much attention to aging—he just lets it happen and does the best he can with each and every day. When asked to what he credits living such a long healthy life, he quickly responds with a chuckle, "Not dying!" But he also says that he stays engaged with life. He finds it continually interesting and has no plans to ever give up.

"I haven't given up because I like interesting things. I like to read, but only non-fiction. I don't waste my time on things people make up—whether it's television, movies, or books. I like the true stuff; learning new and interesting things keeps me going."

He also keeps himself going by taking good care of himself. "I walk every day to keep me limber because I don't want to become one of those people who sits around so long that they can't move even if they try," Bill said. "I do sit-ups and walk up and down my mobilehome steps about three hundred times—that seems to keep me vertical. I don't take any medications, and my doctors say they don't understand me—that they've never seen anyone like me. I take that as a compliment!"

While his daily routine helps keep him healthy, being independent, definitely keeps him happy. He still drives his own car and passes his driving examination every year with keen eyes and steady hands, the ones that have played such an essential part in Bill's entire life plan. "You've got to keep going on the highway of life—just keep driving forward: it's all part of the plan!"

Bertha Holt, 94

Eugene, Oregon

She believes that God has guided her and taught her one of life's most important lessons: to take care of others. And with fourteen children—six by birth and eight adopted—seventeen grandchildren, and literally thousands of other children around the world who call her Grandma, Bertha is definitely helping in God's work.

"My husband and I started an adoption agency forty-two years ago to help children in orphanages around the world find homes and families to share their love with," Bertha said. "We have children from fourteen different

countries, including Korea, China, Thailand, India, the Philippines, Guatemala, and many, many other places."

This whole enterprise began when Bertha and her husband attracted national media attention in their efforts to adopt eight Korean children. As it turned out, all eight arrived in the United States on the same day! It was a tremendous undertaking for the Holts—Bertha's husband, Harry, had to stay in Korea for five months, while Bertha worked at gaining passage of a law in the United States. Although there was red tape to deal with, appropriate laws were passed, and soon other families became interested in following in the Holts' footsteps and sought out their guidance.

"We found ourselves deeply involved in helping others adopt children from foreign country orphanages, and that's how our agency got started. Although we've made numerous sacrifices to achieve this, we continue to bring children and families together . . . and that is clearly worth all the sacrifices." Many may wonder how a nonagenarian still does it all, but according to Bertha, it's very simple: "God decided to let me live a long life, and I'm just making the best of it."

Although Bertha believes she's been blessed with good genes, since both of her parents also lived well into their nineties, she also takes good care of herself. She works hard, is passionate about her work, and also thinks the daily 1¼-mile run she's been doing for the past twenty-seven years has helped, too.

"I don't know if you could exactly call it a run—but I get out there and move it every day," Bertha laughed. "I even hold the world record for my age—of course, there wasn't anyone else running against me, but a win is a win, I guess! People do seem a bit surprised that I can still do it, but maybe it will help inspire others."

Bertha believes that too often people get older and just let their bodies stop. She sees no benefit in that and says she'll continue to keep going until she can't go anymore. Although she suffered a mild stroke last year, she feels fortunate that it did not incapacitate her other than messing up her handwriting a bit. This is challenge enough, however, because she writes about twenty-five letters a week, corresponding with all the children in her life. Bertha knows that her exercise routine is probably the main reason the stroke was as mild as it was and that it's also God's plan for her to continue sharing her work.

"I think it's so important to have joy and happiness in one's life," Bertha said. "I know I'm happy with my life and believe that has contributed to my longevity, too. We are put here to live life for others, not to get so caught up in just our own lives that we forget about everything else. Unfortunately, I think that as people get older they get so absorbed and overwhelmed with all of their own problems and changes that they often get depressed—because they have no other focus."

So focusing on others is exactly what Bertha does . . . it's what she's always done, and it's what she'll always do.

David Hopkins, 72, and Jim Stegall, 67

San Diego, California

When you talk about an adventure, how does a 12,000-mile trek through the mountains, back country, and remote villages of South America sound? It was a three-month journey of experiencing youth hostels, mingling with the locals, living with Indians on an island with no electricity or running water, traveling mostly on trains and buses—and one more minor detail, both Jim and David are legally blind.

"When I first proposed the trip to David, he reacted with a burst of laughter and thought I was crazy!" Jim said. "Being blind, the thought of us doing this type of trip without the aid of a sighted person initially seemed like an insurmountable challenge. But after he had time to think about it, he recognized that this offered us the opportunity to put a positive connotation on our blindness—to turn it away from being a handicap."

And that's exactly what they did. Because both Jim and David had been diagnosed with retinitis pigmentosa, a genetic degenerative disease of the eye, they decided to combine their adventure with a little fund-raising as well. They solicited more than 130 sponsors and raised $10,000 for the Foundation for Fighting Blindness.

Their adventure actually began the moment they stepped on the plane. The extent of their planning was a round-trip ticket—they had no reservations for any part of the trip and didn't even know where they were going to spend their first night. Additionally, they spoke very little Spanish, and although David's was better than Jim's, communication would be a challenge. They also discovered early in their journey that no one recognized them as being legally blind: white canes were a foreign concept. Fortunately, however, people did recognize that they needed some assistance and were friendly enough to help out.

"It was a struggle at first—we'd go through doors and knock each other down, but by the third day anywhere the locals were looking after us, taking our arms to help us wherever we went," Jim said.

The people they met and the experiences they shared made this the adventure of a lifetime. One of their most memorable ones was the train ride from the top of the Andes, in the city of Alausi, to the city of Bucay, Ecuador, a scenic 11,000 foot drop to sea level, from their view seats on top of the boxcar, with all the locals.

"That was really something!" David exclaimed. "There was no one our age riding up there, just young backpackers from all over the world and the locals; everyone else was seated inside the car down below. But here we were, two blind guys, including one with a hip replacement, climbing up along the catwalk to the top of the train and enjoying the ride. It was quite an experience!"

Jim and David spent the majority of their time in small towns, which they found much more user-friendly. The big cities were complicated and difficult to get around in easily. They specifically remember one incident in Bogota, the capital of Colombia, which had lots of traffic and no crosswalks—so getting across the street became a real challenge.

"I didn't know how we were going to do it without taking our lives in our hands," David said. "While we were assessing the situation, I noticed a nice little old lady and thought that if we stood next to her and went when she did, then we just might make it across . . . and we did!" he laughed.

Fortunately, they didn't encounter any major traumas—challenges aplenty, but nothing too serious to overcome. One of their most exciting challenges occurred when they stayed with a native Indian family at Lake Titicaca, the highest navigable lake in the world at 12,000 feet, on the border between Peru and Bolivia. The island has no electricity, television, telephones, toilets, or running water, and while out on an excursion to the village square—David and Jim made a wrong turn.

"We started out too late so it was getting dark quickly, and at that elevation the temperature falls fast,"

Jim remembered. "We knew something was wrong, that we had somehow made a wrong turn and the thought of being found frozen to death the next day, did cross our minds. Eventually we came across a young boy from the village who only spoke the local dialect. We repeated the name of the family we were staying with and fortunately he understood and guided us back safely."

In addition to the great experience of the adventure itself, it was also a tremendous personal accomplishment for both David and Jim. First and foremost, they were able to come back as friends after spending so much time together and in some very trying situations. But equally important, each learned a lot about himself.

"Covering twelve-thousand total miles, seven countries—Colombia, Ecuador, Peru, Bolivia, Chile, Argentina, and Brazil—and crossing the Straits of Magellan in an old WWII landing craft is an adventure unlike any organized tour," David said. "We experienced the real benefits of being independent—having to rely only on ourselves and each other enabled us to recognize a new-found confidence and ability that transferred right over to our lives back home. To grow, you have to put yourself in challenging situations like this and believe you can do it, and we did!"

"I think we both came back more aware of the fact that we don't know what lies around the corner, both visually or within our own lives," Jim said. "But whatever it is, we'll be able to deal with it."

Donald J. Hubbard, 70

Vista, California

D on trained youth swim teams for thirty-six years, but when time came to do his own training at age 64, he discovered he was only exercising, not training, and there's a big difference between the two.

"The first and probably most important thing I learned was to restructure my training schedule," Don said. "Instead of going hard five days a week, I work out strenuously only three days a week. On the alternate days, I cross-train with yoga and light weightlifting, and the difference has been remarkable!"

Don recognizes that people are often motivated to start a new exercise routine but then find out that enthusiasm can have a price. They may do too much or do it incorrectly, finding themselves in worse shape than before they started. Additionally, he feels it's essential to

discuss exercise plans with a doctor first to make sure the body is as ready as the mind.

"I read a lot on the subject of exercise and aging. There's some excellent new information, and the changes have been rather significant—there's a lot to learn, or relearn, in my case."

Yoga is on his recommended list because it improves flexibility and helps prevent injury. Flexibility, however, decreases with age which makes people feel like they have stiff muscles. Actually it's not the muscles that become stiff—it's the ligaments and tendons that connect to the bones. If they don't get stretched, they can cause added pressure on the joints making them more susceptible to pain and injury. The other age-related change Don experienced was in strength training. He just couldn't do it like he used to, and by continuing to try without making adjustments, he developed shoulder problems as a result. Don quickly learned that the amount of weight being lifted was less important than the number of repetitions.

Don put these new lessons to good use. By lowering the amount of weight and increasing the reps, he could train without pain. However, it was a little too late because he had already developed tendinitis in his shoulder from overdoing it. "That was a hard lesson to learn, because I was knocked him out of swim competition for more than a year. Before I really understood the changes that had to be made in training with age, I simply overdid it by trying to do what I used to and didn't give my body the proper time to heal and recover."

Strength-training studies are relatively new, particularly regarding the aging process. Results from Tufts University in Boston and the Cooper Institute in Dallas indicate that although muscle loss occurs with age, exercise can reverse, slow down, and even prevent this loss. "I've learned there's no age barrier in the ability to build muscle and strength. It's essential to include weights in your workout—the key is to be careful, go slow, and perhaps most importantly, learn how to do it right from the start."

Don obviously knows what he's doing now, because he's winning lots of swimming medals. He recently competed in six events at the National Masters Championships in Florida and came home with a gold, two silver, and three bronze medals. However, Don's proudest moment was his gold-medal win in the 200-meter individual medley (the butterfly, backstroke, breaststroke and crawl) at the United States National Senior Sports Classic VI (Senior Olympics).

Without question Don credits much of his new success to the revised training routine he's incorporated into the second half of his life: swim, stretch and strength. "As you get older you have to deal with some loss, but if you can slow down that loss and prevent injuries, then the losses aren't as bad. I can swim as fast now as I did six years ago because I'm in better physical condition. You have to stay current and informed about what works and what doesn't."

You're never too old to learn something new and there's always something new to learn!

Frank Hyde, 80

Somis, California

They say he's a legend at taking a quarter horse through the course. And folks who know him would never say he's too old to compete, because he still has the reflexes and speed of people one-quarter his age—and the accolades to prove it.

Frank is an octogenarian equestrian who has never let age get in the way of doing what he loves to do: riding horses and competing in Ggymkhana. Maneuvering horses through an obstacle course featuring quick turns and barrel racing is based on speed and agility, not the rider's age. Frank's still among the fiercest competitors around, and he's been around a long time. "I can't remember when I wasn't riding a horse," Frank said. "I've been doing this for decades and since I still enjoy it, I see no reason to stop."

He's the oldest competitor of the 3,000-member California Gymkhana Association and still one of the best. Frank continues to compete in the top-echelon events, too, the AAA+, which is the sport's fastest division.

"Speed is the key, and that lies in the horse," Frank explained. "I don't just use any type of quarter horse: these are racetrack caliber—Gymkhana requires a fast horse in order to win."

And win he does. In fact, he's made the state Hall of Fame twice—both times at an age with million-to-one odds that he couldn't. "I was pushing 70 when I did it—so I was pretty old then—but not too old to do it! I'm proud, because it's tough—each year about thirty sign up and only a handful ever make it, so it's quite an honor to succeed."

Frank has succeeded in other ways besides his Gymkhana competitions. He's led clinics for children during summer vacations and holidays, as well as coached hundreds of students, which he says is the most rewarding. "It's a real special feeling for me to see so many of the kids I've taught still competing and enjoying the sport. I'm proud to say I've trained a number of the top riders, and I know I've taught them to respect the sport, too, and that's important for its future."

Frank leads by example and is a tribute to the image of the gentleman cowboy: clean-cut, handsomely dressed in a starched shirt, with a bola tie (not required), boots, jeans, with a big shiny silver belt buckle often

representing a recent victory. He's the consummate professional and is highly respected in his field.

"It's important for the kids to learn the etiquette of the sport as much as the sport itself," Frank said. "It had a bad image several years ago—redneck, long-hair, baseball-hat-wearing guys with a beer in one hand and the reins in the other. Fortunately, though, the Association has set new standards and rules for competition, so it's a true gentleman's sport again."

This is not to say it's only a sport for men—Frank has taught his share of women riders as well. Regardless of whether they're men or women, Frank's students love to compete, and oftentimes it's a real thrill when they meet again back in the ring. "I still compete against a number of my students, and regardless of who wins, it's fun being out there and seeing them enjoy it—that's a guaranteed victory for me every time!"

Frank credits his personal life to much of his success. He's been married to his wife, Clara, for forty-seven years, has three children, four grandchildren, and three great-grandchildren . . . who all know how to ride. He's preparing to ship one of his own horses to a granddaughter and great-granddaughter in Texas, so the legacy lives on.

"I'll be riding as long as possible, and considering I'm still pretty young at 80—I've got no plans to ride off into that sunset yet!"

Ella Jenkins, 73

Chicago, Illinois

The delicate sound of a songbird chirping its morning tune is brought to life as Ella performs her musical magic. The enchanting storytelling is about to begin as she shares legendary tales from all over the world with children of all ages. It's a labor of love and a contribution of spirit—and it's Ella's gift, which she gives every day.

Ella is fascinating. Her ability to transcend generations and cultures, blending music and storytelling together, is a genuine passion that has become a lifelong commitment. "I believe communication is so important—and with children it has to be fun, so I blend music and storytelling together in a way that encourages them to interact with me while we learn about the past, experience other cultures, and explore their own rhythms in a special and unique way."

Ella's style is quite unique, and it captivates the hearts of young and old alike. She has performed concerts on all seven continents and is often recognized from her work on *Sesame Street, Barney,* and *Mister Rogers' Neighborhood,* as well as from her videos and countless recordings for the Smithsonian/Folkways label.

"Children are my favorite people because of their innocence, sincerity, and genuine trusting nature," Ella said. "They come to hear the lady sing—the familiar voice, story, or song they remember—without thinking in terms related to color, sex, size, or age. There's a lot we can learn from children, and by interacting with them we often discover new things about ourselves."

Her programs are as educational as they are enjoyable, and through her talent at combining music and story-telling, she involves the children in a lesson of language and culture that mesmerizes all who are fortunate enough to experience her magic. "I bring the children onto the stage with me, and together we play instruments I've gathered from cultures all over the world. I teach them about the rhythms from these various places and encourage them to experience the culture by playing the instruments themselves. Whether it's a Nairobi shaking basket, tambourine, harmonica, or clapsticks made by Australian aborigines, the children connect in a way that is both special and powerful. You can see it on their faces as they explore these new worlds with openness and curiosity."

Involving the children directly in her program is a priority for Ella. "It becomes a lesson in self-esteem as I encourage children to be themselves and find their own natural rhythm," she said. "Childhood is such a wonderful period in life, particularly if kids are allowed to experience it without the constant pushing to advance. It's better to instead just let them naturally learn to be themselves—and like it!"

Ella believes there is too much emphasis today on achievements rather than experiences, which she feels are the real foundation for living. "Experiences should be the focus, because change is a way of life, just like rhythms are. For example, with aging . . . we don't seem to be able to accept age as a natural rhythm change and instead always seem to fight it by believing the image has to be perfect, as is evident with the growth in businesses that strive for 'eternal youth' through makeup, plastic surgery, and other methods."

She does recognize, however, that her work has per-haps even more significance because of her age. Ella feels it is extremely important for children to have the opportunity to interact with an older person—some-thing she believes is missing in too many of their lives. "If children don't have the opportunity to be around older people, they may become frightened when they see a gray-haired person, just because they've never been exposed to one before. But when they have the op-portunity to interact and spend time together—the magic happens on its own."

A spiritual connection is also important in Ella's life. Every day she thanks God for all the blessings in her life and the opportunity to make a difference in someone else's life. "Life's about loving others, sharing, caring, and giving, and a person's age has little to do with that," Ella says. She's aware of her age, but doesn't dwell on it and doesn't want to be categorized by it. It's not the number of years we live, but what we do with those years that really matters.

"It's about continuing to contribute something to the world we live in and giving of ourselves to others. If I can pass that on to those I encounter along my path, children and adults alike, then my time here will have been well spent."

Kearney Johnston, 87

San Diego, California

I f you're looking for a quick way to feel younger, do what Kearney does—hop in a boat! Kearney says he feels like he goes from age 87 to 27 by doing his daily sculling and believes that it, combined with clean living, will beat the aging thing every time.

Kearney knows a lot about winning and aging, considering he's the oldest competitive rower in the United States. He's been an active member of the San Diego Rowing Club since his first competition in 1930, sixty-seven years ago. Few have the dedication he's shown for the sport and his fellow rowers. Kearney's coached and taught the art of sculling to more than nine-hundred people—without every charging them a dime. One of his students even went to the Olympic games!

"Some people call me a legend . . . and I guess I may be by now!" laughed Kearney. "If you do something long enough, that's what happens . . . but it's still fun and I believe it keeps me healthy, too, so why stop now?"

Although he is a tenacious and fierce competitor in the water, one of the main reasons Kearney is still sculling today is the gentle impact this form of exercise has on the body. As a result, it may be one of the best exercises one can do over a lifetime.

"Sculling works the muscles, helps with balance, and definitely has cardiovascular benefits, too," Kearney said. "I use two sculls that I refer to as telephone poles, because I'm old-fashioned and still use the wooden ones . . . most everyone else uses the lightweight fiberglass sculls. Pulling these sculls through the water provides good resistance work for the muscles, and balance can improve, too, because you have to keep the boat on an even keel, being careful not to rock it with wasted motion."

Of course, Kearney is one who sees no benefit in wasting anything, and certainly not time. His days typically begin at 4 A.M. with a bite to eat, and he's generally long gone before the morning newspaper even arrives. "I usually get to the club around 6 or 6:30 A.M., depending on whether I have a ride that day or if it's my one day to take the bus. Once I'm there, I distribute the mail, sweep the sand out of the men's locker room, and am generally in the water by 7 or 7:30 A.M."

Kearney prefers to row double, with a partner, and says that oftentimes he finds himself coaching right there on-site. Even with a bad back, he's still out there every day. First he rows a gentle two miles on the early morning glass and calm water conditions, followed by a hard thousand meters to check his strokes. Then it's a tough 550 meters in rough water due to choppy seas created by water-skiers later in the morning, but that doesn't bother Kearney. It creates a challenge, and he says it makes for an extra good workout.

"By the time I'm done with my workout I'm ready for breakfast again, and hopefully I'll talk a few folks into joining me for French toast. Then it's back home to read the paper and see what's going on in the world, part of my mental workout to keep me current on what's happening."

Kearney does love his sport, and those in the sport love Kearney, too. He's inspired people of all ages and many are amazed he's still at it. Kearney says he knows the secret . . . it's sculling that keeps him alive!

Dr. Margaret H. Jones, 93

Pacific Palisades, California

D r. Margaret H. Jones has a passion for life. Professionally, she is recognized as a pioneer in the treatment of cerebral palsy. For her extraordinary, sixty-five year career dedicated to improving the lives of both children and adult CP patients in the United States, she received the first Lifetime Achievement Award from the United Cerebral Palsy/Spastic Children's Foundation of Los Angeles and Ventura Counties.

Margaret was one of only a handful of women to graduate from Cornell Medical School in 1933. In the field of CP research, she is credited with recognizing the need to treat infants early with daily therapy. Margaret also initiated the philosophy of comprehensive care for CP treatment, addressing the need to treat all of the patient's symptoms in an attempt to improve their total quality of life.

Today she still hasn't stopped. She continues to serve as an advocate for people with cerebral palsy and thoroughly believes there is still much work to be done. Margaret contributes in her typically devoted way— every week she hitches a ride to UCLA to volunteer her services at the CP clinic, where she is sought out by physicians for her input on a variety of specialty cases.

Beyond her professional life, there is a vibrant individual who has a true love for and understanding of the real meaning of life. "My desire is to always keep growing . . . staying involved is what life is all about. I've always believed life is what you make it, and we should make the most of it. That's why my contributions will continue throughout my entire life."

One of the most beautiful things in Margaret's life, occurred at the age of 84, when she entered into her first (and only) marriage, to Dr. Adrian C. Kanaar. "I was never really looking to fall in love, but I also hadn't given up on the possibility either. I hoped I would meet 'Mr. Right' someday—it just took a little longer to find him. But Adrian was certainly worth the wait."

They met at church, through their minister, and both knew instantly this was something special. She describes a feeling of magic they both shared, which continued throughout their short time together. "When we met—sparks flew! He was indeed a true blessing in my life. Our partnership was one of total unity . . . we shared so much in common, and each and every day we spent together was a wonderful gift I will always cherish."

Margaret was a beautiful bride and celebrated with all the typical traditions. She excitedly made the plans for their wedding day, had bridal showers and even shopped for the perfect wedding gown. As it turned out, she had it specially made by the daughter-in-law of one of her favorite pediatrician colleagues.

"The gown was exquisite . . . long and white with a lovely train, and a delicate veil," Margaret said. "The flowers, the guest list, the music, the ceremony were all so wonderful . . . just like every bride's dream. We had bridesmaids, grooms-men, and children from the bell choir performed the music—which was absolutely angelic. One thing about getting married later in life, however, is that there are a lot of guests—we had more than three hundred in the church, so it was indeed a day of special memories of a glorious occasion."

Their newlywed life was similar to any other, according to Margaret. She knows this may be surprising, but she believes it's important for people to know that inti-

macy is lifelong and is something that people can experience and enjoy all their lives, regardless of chronological age. "He too had a background in medicine, so we shared scientific interests as well as social and environmental issues. We both enjoyed reading and every morning read the Bible together. We loved hiking and did a fair amount before his health declined. He came to my sixtieth college reunion, and I accompanied him to England for one of his. It was indeed a beautiful union that I will always be very thankful for."

They were only able to share four short years together before Adrian died in 1993, but he will never be forgotten, because Margaret created the Jones-Kanaar Foundation in his memory. Dedicated to youth and assisting people with CP, the foundation supports programs for the physically challenged and grants awards for volunteerism at local high schools. Additionally, Margaret's most recent venture is the development of the *Reading Picture Book for Toddlers*, because she believes that children can learn an amazing amount in the first three years of life with appropriate learning tools and good parent-child bonding.

"There is still much to do to improve the lives of others. Whether it's through my activities in the church and my community or the research projects for CP, the importance of continuing to contribute and make things happen is what inspires me to keep doing every day. Mental stimulation is so essential throughout our lives, and once you give that up and lose interest in the world around you, it's all downhill from there."

Dr. Margaret Jones-Kanaar is one who makes things happen, and she has no intention of stopping her contributions anytime soon. Engagement keeps you connected to life . . . and life is definitely her true passion.

Cam Jones, 87

Piedmont, California

He's always been athletic but just never had the time to participate the way he wanted to . . . until retirement. Cam's philosophy is if he's going to do something, he might as well do it right. Which is what he's done with rowing. A very humble man, Cam has won numerous national and masters championships but says it's the joy of participation that matters most.

"My father was an oarsman at Cal Berkeley, so I guess it's in my genes. I tried it once in college, but I just didn't have the physique they were looking for . . . too small. So I've always been intrigued with the sport, I just got into it a little later than most. I was actually in my sixties by the time I got serious about it, and it's been a great ride ever since. I've competed for over twenty years now, and hope to keep doing it for another twenty more!"

Cam was always mesmerized by the rowers out on Lake Merritt, a spot where he and his wife of fifty-eight years, Danne, would go for walks, to feed the ducks, and soak up nature's ambience. The synchronized rowers' strokes looked like absolute poetry, and it seemed like a sport that could be done at any age and speed.

"Sculling involves simple, smooth movements," Cam said. "It's not about jumping around or colliding with others; it's a beautiful, soothing sport that is as therapeutically beneficial as it is physically beneficial. Age isn't an issue in sports; it just comes into play in competition, as far as what division you're in. Age shouldn't stop you from participating in anything, and I think that's what I've shown some of the younger kids. We all

147

go to the same regattas together—I just compete in a different division. We're always happy for each other when anyone wins a medal!"

One of the main features that attracted Cam to this sport in his later years was the ability to work out at various levels. Although Cam's participation in rowing over the past twenty years has been very physical, the last two years have been a time where his participation has been more concentrated in the sport's therapeutic benefits. "The doctors said I was at risk for a heart attack, so I had preventive surgery two years ago to replace a valve. In some respects I feel worse now than before the surgery. The scar tissue that developed as a result of the surgery, blocked my right ventricle and significantly reduced my cardiovascular ability. It took me a year to get back in the boat, but I got there. I worked up to rowing three times a week and eventually competed in the Masters Nationals rowing doubles, and we even won!"

Cam is a champion, and champions know what it takes to get through adversity. He's never been one to give up and believes challenges are good for building character. "I don't mind being limited a bit; I can accept that. I intend to be alive until at least age 95 and I'm going to use my body as much as I can, within reason, of course. I can still compete and do it well, so I know I'll be O.K. It's just a new phase for me that I'm getting used to. I still get out on the lake and row my boat, and that will always make me happy in my heart!"

Payton Jordan, 81

Los Altos, California

He is a true champion in every sense of the word. He's the coach of coaches and the master of the Masters, as he continues to set world records on the track. A source of true inspiration and American pride, Payton has enjoyed great success as an athlete. First as a world-class sprinter at the University of Southern California, and today as a sprint world-record holder with more than twenty-two Masters records. He recently set a world record for the 80-plus age group in the 100-meter dash with a time of 14.35 seconds!

Payton seemed destined to be a champion. He was featured on the cover of *Life* magazine as captain of USC's NCAA championship track team and halfback on

its Rose Bowl winning football team. After graduation, Payton continued his sprint into the history books. Pursuing a place on the Olympic team, Payton won the 1941 National AAU 100-meter championship in 10.3 seconds—a time that equaled the unofficial record set by Jesse Owens. That same year he also set world records of 9.5 seconds in the 100-yard, and 21.1 seconds in the 220-yard on grass. His 100-yard record stood for an amazing twenty-seven years! And although he was definitely on the fast track towards the Olympics, America had other plans for Payton—World War II robbed him of the opportunity.

Payton never gave up, and eventually made it to the Olympics in 1968, as our country's track team coach at the games held in Mexico City. He trained and inspired the athletes to attain a level never seen before. They won more medals and established more records than any other team in history, returning home with twenty-four medals, twelve of which were gold.

And so began Payton's next phase of track and field fame as a coach. For forty years, he devoted his life to the athletes he trained and became one of the world's most respected track and field coaches. After ten years at Occidental College where he coached track and football, including a starting quarterback by the name of Jack Kemp, who went on to the pros and then into politics. Payton spent the next twenty-eight years as the head coach at Stanford University, where he finished his career and now serves as track coach emeritus.

"After I retired, I had some free time to play with so I decided to get back into running," Payton said. "When you reach 50, you've got to look at the next fifty years and ask yourself what you're going to do. I had stayed in good shape, and track is something that I truly love. When are you too old to do anything that makes you happy?"

It's obvious indeed that track makes Payton happy. After a thirty-year absence from competition, Payton made a comeback that is nothing short of phenomenal. He has competed in Masters competitions every year since 1972, when he ran in his first "old-timers" race at the age of 55. In Payton's first year of masters competition, he set world records in the 100-yard, 220-yard, and 200-meter distances. Since then, Payton has lowered the world age-group records in the 100- and 200-meter sprints on an annual basis. "It's not about winning, it's the joy of competition and being blessed with the opportunity to do what I love. I've never been one to project myself as number one—I just go out and do the best that I can with what God's given me."

In addition to being thankful for his athletic abilities, Payton is also very thankful for his family and the love of his life, his wife Marge, with whom he has shared fifty-seven years. She is the ultimate joy in his life, and when she fell ill Payton officially retired, spending two years away from the track in order to help her heal. "There are certain priorities in one's life, and family will always be my top concern. It was a good break because I never could have concentrated on running knowing she was sick. So I just hung 'em up, and when I did decide to come back, it was only because Marge got better. Plus, conveniently enough, the Masters was held in the Bay area for the first time—so being in my own backyard, it was just too good to pass up."

Payton says he uses the same philosophy today in his training as he always has. The only major difference now is the increased amount of rest required before races. He's never been one of those fanatics whose daytime uniform is a pair of shorts and running shoes. In fact, he doesn't do any more running than he has to because it puts too much strain on the joints. He continues to do lots of flexibility exercises and stretching, and it's evident that this routine works well, since he's been virtually injury-free.

Payton is firmly committed to enjoying the quality of life, not just the quantity. Some of his favorite activities are also beneficial exercises for track. "I love gardening—it's very therapeutic physically and emotionally," Payton said. "Being in the yard with nature, the flowers, and earth's soil is very healthy and invigorating for me. I guess it's part of the nurturing that is such a strong part of my being, just like with coaching—it's a wonderful feeling watching things grow and tending to their efforts," Payton philosophized. Finding joy in whatever you do, Payton believes, is one of the most essential aspects of growing older in a healthy, vital way. He says it doesn't matter what the activity is, as long as it brings that zest and happiness to your life. Without it, he believes life loses some of its meaning.

"I am so thankful to have activities that I so thoroughly enjoy and ones I can be involved with in a variety of capacities. I may not be running for the rest of my life, but you can be assured I'll be involved with track in some capacity. Aging is about growing—we don't just get old, and we don't just stop growing because we're older. If you do, then you're giving up, and that's a problem."

Payton believes it's an exciting time to be growing older. Extraordinary breakthroughs in scientific and medical research have enabled people to live longer, healthier, and more active lives. "Our generation is really on the cutting edge, and we can be role models to those younger than ourselves. Retirement does not mean sitting down, doing and saying nothing. Why waste the wisdom, creativity, energy, and God-given gifts? We must continually create lives of value by meeting daily challenges. Nothing ever just happens . . . we have to make it happen," Payton said. "So life is what we make it, and we should always experience the moment and the joy of living a vital and rewarding life all through our years."

Spoken like a true champion. Payton forever will be in the record books as an inspiration to us all.

Wally Jordan, 76

Prescott Valley, Arizona

L ife's a rush to Wally, an adrenaline rush that's
been one heck of a ride. He rides motorcycles farther and longer than just about anyone his age.
Ego, motivation, and determination drive him, and he
says driving those bikes is what keeps him young.

Wally's been riding motorcycles since 1944. In his
youth, it was mostly off-road dirt bike riding. In his professional life, he rode street bikes as an undercover
Deputy Sheriff in Orange County, California. There he
rode with several of the toughest gangs in the Laguna
Beach area. Now that he's in retirement, he rides for endurance and distance.

"You can't talk about endurance without talking
about determination—riding is about 40 percent ability
and 60 percent determination to endure what it takes to
make a long ride," Wally said. "Age has nothing to do
with it because all my records have been achieved after
age 71. In fact, age may actually work in my favor, because over time I've developed the discipline and know
what it takes to do what I say I'm going to do."

Wally's first organized long-distance ride was the
famous Four Corners Rally that requires touching all four
corners of the United States in twenty-one days or less.
Wally decided to add a new twist to the event and became
the first and oldest to ever do a round trip! He started in
San Diego, traveled up to the Washington-Canadian border, across the country to the upper tip of Maine, and then
south to Key West, Florida. In Key West he bought fuel,
took a photo to document his arrival, made a U-turn, and
went right back the way he came, finishing in San Diego

and completing the entire 14,500-mile round-trip in just 19 ½ days—an amazing new record.

"I don't know which part is more amazing—the fact that I did it, the fact that I was 71, or the fact that I did it on a nontraditional street bike. I rode a Suzuki DR650, which is really more like a dirt bike, and no one ever believed it was possible—but it was, because I did it, and now I get the last laugh!"

Wally became a celebrity in the process. Suzuki found out about the ride, and as a result, a small radio campaign was created in New York called, "Where's Wally?" Listeners were encouraged to keep an eye out for Wally on the roadways, and if they saw him on his bike, they could call in and win a prize. As it turned out, Wally was the one who won the prize, because Suzuki was so impressed with his accomplishment that they presented him with a brand-new motorcycle for his efforts.

The Guinness Book of World Records offered another intriguing challenge that Wally knew he could do: ride a motorcycle from the Atlantic to the Pacific, 2,373 miles in less than forty-two hours. He started in Jacksonville, Florida and rode all the way to San Diego in forty hours and ten minutes! Although he had clearly broken the record, Guinness declined to honor it because he was not under "unremitting surveillance." "My name's not in print for accomplishing it, but I know I did it and that's good enough for me. Besides, it's the adventure along the way and the experience of doing it that really matters anyway. I did what I said I'd do: I reached and surpassed the goal I set for myself, and that's the real accomplishment."

Since then there have been even more accomplishments, including a ride to forty-eight states which took nine days and four hours; a 1,701-mile ride in twenty-three hours and fifty minutes; numerous 1500-mile rides in less than twenty-four hours; and a first- and fourth-place finish in the Alberta, Canada 2000-plus kilometer endurance rides where he competed against sixty serious riders from across the United States and Canada. All were considerably younger than he with an average age of 45—the next closest person to Wally's age was only 60. "Achieving a goal has little to do with age, except that when you're younger, I think it's easier to quit—at least it was for me. I enjoy the feeling of succeeding, and working hard for something always makes the victory that much sweeter."

Wally firmly believes determination and motivation are the most important secrets in life. Unfortunately, he feels too few know how to use these traits to their advantage to reach their full potential. The combination of the two is tough to beat, and once you implement them in your life, you'll discover why Wally believes they are the traits that drive him.

Aging's a rush—and it could just be the ride of your life, too.

Rev. Dr. Paul C. Klose, 83

Sanbornton, New Hampshire

It's quite a compliment when people you haven't seen for years say you look just like you used to or that you haven't changed a bit. And it's even more extraordinary when you're an octogenarian, and people still tell you this. Rev. Paul seems to have the aging process in control beyond just taking good care of himself—he even went back to school at the age of 82 to study gerontology!

"In my graduate courses, instructors always seemed to emphasize the importance of planning for the future," said Rev. Paul. "So when I got to 'the future' point in my life, I got educated about the aging process beyond just my own personal experience with the subject. I'm now the oldest graduate in gerontology from the New Hampshire Technical College."

Rev. Paul shares his lessons with others by giving talks about "Turning Back the Biological Clock," and "The Secrets of Staying Young," to people in nursing homes, retirement communities, senior centers, and anywhere else that will have him. "People are intrigued with ways to stay young while growing older. Gerontology is so new that even though more and more people are growing older, as a society, we are still not quite sure about this aging news. Is it really something we have control over? If so, how does one age in a healthy, active, vital, and productive way?" To answer these and other aging questions, Rev. Paul has developed a list of five specific factors he believes makes a difference in the way people age.

"The first is goals. People need to have goals all through their lives, and it doesn't change just because you get older. Having something to look forward to, a reason to get up in the morning, something to strive for and be involved with, is important at any age."

"The second is attitude. Stay positive and beware of pessimism. It can creep into your life and before you know it, the glass is half empty instead of half full. Try to be an optimist—it will help make you feel better and may actually make a difference in your physical health, too. Studies are connecting the role our mind plays in in-fluencing our health, and with aging it's no different. In fact, since aging is perceived so negatively by most peo-ple, this attitude may actually have an adverse effect on our health as we grow older," said Rev Paul.

"The third is a sense of humor. Laughter is good medicine for the body, mind, and soul. I always encour-age people to smile and have fun every day. "Fourth, think of others and focus less on yourself, your needs, your problems, and your issues. When you start think-ing of others, you forget about some of your own aches and pains. People often say they feel a great sense of joy when they do for others—we really do get more out of giving than receiving!"

"And fifth, is the spiritual side of life. For fifty-one years I served as an ordained American Baptist minister, but I don't preach to people on becoming religious, just about my belief in the importance of having faith and a spiritual connection in their life."

Rev. Paul is obviously still devoted to sharing his message—and it appears it is one that will continue to serve as a blessing to others.

Esther Krieger, 81

Beverly Hills, California

At least Esther is honest about it—if she didn't teach her exercise class, she knows she wouldn't have the discipline to go on her own. Whatever the reason, it's worked, because she's been doing this for more than twenty years!

Esther believes most people lack the motivation and personal discipline required to benefit from regular exercise. She's also very familiar with the aches and pains that seemingly come with age. They were what contributed to her initial interest in leading an exercise class for older adults, who may have slowed down a bit but, want to do something about it.

"The golden years take a lot of hard work, and exercise is part of it," Esther said. "It's not about helping people live longer as much as it is about making today and tomorrow good days, and this class seems to make a difference in that outcome."

Much more than exercise takes place in these classes: there's camaraderie, friendship, support, and laughter, which attendees seem to benefit from as much as the exercise. In fact, Esther even prepares a roll sheet for everyone with the name and phone number of each member listed so people can stay in touch and make plans to get together outside of class. "I think the social element of these classes is just as important as the physical exercise. I'm not just teaching exercise—I like to stress the whole person, and since we are all similar in age, it's likely we have issues in common that we can help support each other with."

160

Some of Esther's students have been with her since the beginning. She believes the main reason people continue to come is because they feel better when they do and notice the difference when they don't. She thinks the real determining factor is deciding how you want to spend this part of your life. "I'm not an athlete in any sense of the word, but I know I better move my body," Esther said. "If you want to cater to all the aches and pains—that's your choice. I believe there are things we can do that can make a difference, lessen the pain, and make it all more tolerable."

"I do it selfishly," Esther laughed. "I get such pleasure being in contact with all the special people in my life . . . and doing for others is doing for me, too!"

Tom Krumm, 78

Oceanside, California

Declared "totally disabled" at the young age of 57 due to back problems, who would have believed twenty years later that the backstroke would enable Tom to get back into life again?

"We all make mistakes when we're younger, thinking we're invincible," Tom remembered. "I had back problems most of my life due to a career that involved a lot of heavy lifting, but it was undoubtedly a crash I took on a jet-ski in my early fifties that did the most damage. We were out riding the waves, having a great time and I took some air by jumping a wave. To my surprise I found a sandbar on the other side instead of water. I came crashing down, with my back taking most of the impact."

Tom's crash resulted in a broken back and partial paralysis, which caused not only tremendous pain with any type of movement, but also the need for a back brace for just about anything he did.

It's not too surprising Tom found himself back in the water again, but this time for therapeutic reasons. One of the primary benefits of water therapy is the buoyancy eliminates much of the strain and pressure on the joints which allows people with debilitating conditions to move freely and comfortably again.

"I picked up swimming to help my back heal," said Tom. "The backstroke is excellent for back problems because it helps build up the muscles on both sides of the spine. Your back is in a good rounded position when you perform the stroke correctly. The breaststroke does the opposite by arching your back. I've made remarkable progress . . . I mean, I was literally physically disabled. At first, I remember that swimming was real hard, but the doctors kept encouraging me to do it, take it slowly, and eventually it all worked out well."

Swimming and pool exercises have become a regular part of Tom's days and he believes very strongly in this regimen as a means of staying healthy and active. In fact, he now encourages his wife of fifty-five years, Mary, to also do pool therapy to help her vertigo condition, and it seems to be working.

The benefits of water therapy continue to grow, and its effectiveness has nothing to do with being a good swimmer, but rather about moving the body again in a way that is often more comfortable than on land. The number of older adults who have taken up swimming in recent years indicates that it's an activity that can be performed for much of one's lifetime, without much risk of serious injury. It's an activity that gently works muscles, feels good, and is good for you.

Although Tom battles high blood pressure today, he claims he's in great shape and has little doubt that he's in better shape at 78, than he ever was before the accident. His blood pressure drops a significant twenty to thirty points when measured after his exercise routine and usually stays at a safe level until he gets involved in one of his challenging bridge games! The mental benefits of playing cards seem to balance it all out and all in all . . . he's healthy and happy.

Jack LaLanne, 83

San Luis Obispo, California

We all want to stay healthy, prevent disease, and maintain an activity level of vigor and vitality. But are we willing to do the work, or rather the workout, in order to achieve it? If it's motivation you need, there are few more inspiring than Jack LaLanne. Known to many as the "Godfather of Fitness," Jack continues his commitment to health and wellness in a way that is inspirational to one and all, regardless of age.

Age has obviously not slowed Jack down. He's in great shape, rising daily at 5 A.M. to perform a two-hour workout, followed by a breakfast of carrot-celery juice, banana, apple, and protein powder. He still performs the extraordinarily difficult military-style fingertip push-ups, and his biceps and stomach muscles are hard as rocks—even after all these years. He celebrated his 60th birthday with a two-mile swim across San Francisco Bay, handcuffed and with ankles shackled, tugging a sand-filled one thousand-pound dinghy. For his 70th, he swam a mile through the Long Beach Harbor, again in handcuffs and leg irons, but this time he tugged seventy rowboats, each with an occupant!

"Just because I'm who I am, people think it's easy and that I live to exercise," Jack said. "I do like how I feel and enjoy my good health, but it takes discipline. I have that same little devil sitting on my shoulder, too, constantly giving me excuses to not work out, but I know better. It's an essential part of my life; it energizes me every day. So why not continue doing something that is so beneficial?"

Although he is recognized as the original health and fitness guru, proprietor of the first health club, inventor of weight machines, and originator of the exercise video, Jack didn't start his life out in a very healthy way. In fact, in his youth he called himself a "junk-food junkie". He says that he was actually a sugarholic, but fortunately turned it around after hearing a nutrition lecture that changed his life.

"I was 15 at the time and my poor eating habits were making me weak, mean, and sick. I suffered with all sorts of physical ills, including headaches and bulimia. Sugar in the body is like alcohol. It destroys all the B vitamins, which makes you irritable and unable to think right. I realized that I had a choice in how I felt, so right then and there I made a commitment to change my lifestyle and build a totally new Jack LaLanne!"

Jack studied everything he could get his hands on about nutrition and fitness. He was pre-med in college but graduated as a doctor of chiropractic due to his insatiable interest in helping people with prevention, before they became ill. "I decided to focus on chiropractic because there was more emphasis on the natural methods. My original goal was to become a doctor, but they were more into drugs, drugs, drugs, and I thought there was a better way."

So Jack went right to work on proving there was a better way, and it was exercise. He opened the nation's first heath club in Oakland, California in 1936 at age 21, and named it the Jack LaLanne Physical Culture Studio. Not only was it America's first health spa, but the very first modern health spa in the world. There was nothing else like it, anywhere.

"This was the first progressive exercise studio that actually had people working out with weights, barbells and machines. I was the first to advocate weight resistance training, which is very common now, but it wasn't then. In fact, most people thought I was simply nuts. I forged ahead anyway and developed the first models of exercise equipment that have become standard in today's health spas, including leg-extension machines, pulley machines using cables, and the first weight selectors."

Jack was a pioneer with his crusade to promote the benefits of resistance-training exercises to improve health. He remembers when doctors told people that working out with weights would lead to heart attacks, a lower sex drive, and that women would start to look like men. Today, with the abundance of research touting the benefits of strength training, combined with the growing numbers of world-class athletes who now work out with weights, Jack should be considered as much a visionary as he is a pioneer.

He continued to spread his message about the benefits of exercise through the powerful medium of television: *"The Jack LaLanne Show"* first aired in 1951. Young Jack knew that few people would be enthusiastic about exercising, so he had a gimmick. Happy, a beautiful white German shepherd, appeared with him on the air. Recognizing that children were his initial audience, and that they controlled the television in the morning, he instinctively knew they would love the dog and therefore would watch the show. "That's how we made the show personal, by embracing the kids and encouraging them to go get their mom, dad, grandmother, grandfather, or anybody else who was in the house to come out and exercise with Uncle Jack and Happy on TV. Not wanting to disappoint the kids, the adults exercised too. It was all part of the plan and is really how it all began."

The Jack LaLanne Show aired for eight years and went into national syndication in 1959, where it stayed until 1985. In total, Jack exercised on TV five days a week for thirty-four years! During that time, he also opened his own gyms and franchised a number of spas under the Jack LaLanne name. He has written several books, produced a variety of exercise videos, and still maintains his own business, Be Fit Enterprises, all in support of his efforts to promote health and fitness for people of all ages.

His wife Elaine is also a health and fitness advocate in her own right. She has shared the benefits of exercise with the masses as an instructor, on videos, and in her books. Happily married for thirty-nine years, Jack and Elaine are a team who encourage people to take care of the most important person in the world: themselves.

"The advice is plain and simple, and there are two primary rules," Jack said. "First, if man makes it, don't eat it . . . and if it tastes good, spit it out!" Elaine added, "Jack's as serious about diet as he is about exercise. He is the most disciplined person I've ever met when it comes to eating habits. He will not eat between meals, and he won't eat hors d'oeuvres or even take a bite of birthday cake. We do sometimes enjoy a couple of glasses of wine with our dinner, because in moderation it's supposed to be good for our health."

Jack knows the benefits of a good diet, so he fuels his body with legumes, brown rice, whole-grain bread, lentils, hard-boiled egg whites, olive oil, and fruits. He is also adamant about his vitamins and supplements—he takes "hundreds" of them, including all the antioxidants, vitamin C, alfalfa, watercress, parsley, garlic, and many other herbs as well.

"The second rule is: you've got to make exercise a part of your day—the older you are, the more you should do," Jack said. As a founding member of the Governor's Council on Physical Fitness and Sports, Jack's primary interest is in addressing the large percentage of the population who disdain regular exercise. "We've got to teach people that exercise improves your quality of life by enabling you to live longer and healthier. Education is key, particularly in the area of fitness and aging. Exercise has been proven to delay age-related declines while helping to lessen the pain and debilitation of many conditions people automatically blame on age. It's not necessarily all the fault of age."

Unquestionably still considered by many to be America's health superstar, Jack personifies the secret of healthy aging, and he knows how to keep the body strong and on the go longer. He continues to lead by example and has also maintained his fun sense of humor throughout the process. "We're all interested in saving time, and I think we've found a way to do that—by living longer. Plus, I can't die; it would ruin my image!"

Nate Lazowick, 89

Philadelphia, Pennsylvania

When you reach 89, you're often the oldest in the circles you travel, but that doesn't mean you're old, according to Nate. He doesn't want to be called a senior citizen or treated differently than anyone else—he's as alive as anyone living, and being 89 has nothing to do with being old.

Celebrating at the wedding reception of one of his granddaughters, Nate took a spin on the dance floor and stole the show! Family and friends cheered in response, and called his performance "amazing!"

"What's so 'amazing' about hootin' it up, having a little fun, and letting the music take you back to your youth, with a little dancing?" Nate asked as he laughed. "I guess most people don't think someone my age can still cut up the rug . . . what is it with everyone thinking you fall apart when you get older? That's nonsense!"

Nate knows he's getting older, but he doesn't think he's old. He feels that too often people treat him as if he is old, whether it's family members who wonder if he can make the mile walk to pick up a couple of items at the store, or others who may not even know him. He often wonders what really is normal for aging, because he feels great and believes there needs to be a better understanding about what getting old is all about today. It's obviously different than what most people think.

Perhaps he's developed this unique insight on people's perspectives about aging through his fourteen-year volunteer career with Full Circle, an intergenerational improvisation group at Temple University which specializes in community performances for groups of all ages. The youngest member is a high school junior and Nate's the oldest. The interesting twist is that the troupe has old people playing children and young people playing grandparents.

"I think we've all learned a lot by this—as actors as well as people. I was actually in the audience thirteen years ago when the group performed a skit about a man complaining he had too much time on his hands in retirement and nothing to do. I jumped out of my seat and told the man to get busy and stay busy, thinking they were acting out my life and that is what I needed to do! Fortunately the director of the group liked my enthusiasm and invited me to join . . . I've been there ever since.

Nate encourages others to follow in his footsteps and to get out and get involved. He say's there's a connection to keeping busy and longevity, but also thinks a little old-fashioned luck must play a part in extended healthy living, too. He's had a long, happy sixty-eight year marriage to his wife Sarah, keeps his mind sharp and active by playing a lot of chess, and walks a daily mile or two for exercise to keep his body going.

"I had a quadruple bypass four years ago. I was on a walk when I felt some early symptoms, so I got with my doctor right away and tests confirmed I needed surgery. I've recovered fine, but I also learned how valuable regular checkups are, even when you may feel O.K.—don't wait until you're sick, be prevention-oriented."

Nate sees his doctor every four or five months, takes no medications or vitamins, and claims he feels terrific. He believes that staying active has played a big part in his good health and thinks it's the key to living. "I know too many who punish themselves by saying they're getting older and use that as their reason for not doing something. But I tell them it's all in their head and that they should get out and do something and see if they feel any different after that. Group activities seem especially good, because being with people keeps you involved. Others are counting on you to do your part and celebrate with you when you do!"

So from Nate's perspective, it's all very simple: don't succumb to the problems of age, overcome them. Keep moving, keep thinking, and stop worrying about things. "Be an optimist . . . that's me! My only and worst enemies are time and the calendar. If they weren't invented or discovered, who would know my age? Maybe even I wouldn't know! Besides, age is just a number anyway!"

Ben Levinson, 103

Los Angeles, California

Life's a journey, and it's not the destination that matters as much as the trip along the way. Ben's been on an incredible journey, and he has no plans to fade into the sunset anytime soon. In fact, he intends to ring in the year 2000 because that will mark a special achievement for him, to have lived in three different centuries: the 1800s (Ben was born in 1895); the 1900s; and the next millennium!

"I'm 103-years young, not old!" Ben said. "I'm a recycled teenager. People always want to know how I've lived so long, and I simply tell them—breathe!" he laughed. "But in all seriousness, staying active has been the secret to my long life . . . with a little luck and good fortune added in, too."

Call it luck, call it fate, call it hard work—all play a role in Ben's current challenge: to continue enjoying his independence and quality of life by slowing down the aging process and in some ways actually reversing it. Exercise has been a key component in this effort, but so has an incredible support team who seemed to appear like fate. "I'm not just existing anymore . . . I'm living. I feel better and am stronger now, at 103, than I was at 100. And it's all because of this exercise I'm doing and the new things I've learned."

It all started when a mutual friend introduced Ben to Bob Delaney, 55, a few years ago. With a background in health and fitness, Bob was not only amazed at Ben's abilities at the age of 100, but he was concerned that trouble could be lurking around the bend. "Ben was beginning to have some difficulty walking, which was interfering with the quality of his active lifestyle," Bob said. "He was starting to go downhill primarily due to declining muscle mass in his legs. His balance was off, and he was having a hard time getting up out of a chair. I was confident we could slow down the muscle loss with proper exercise, so I encouraged Ben to give it a try."

Bob told Ben about new research and referred Ben to the book *Biomarkers: The 10 Keys To Prolonging Vitality*, by William Evans, Ph.D., and Irwin H. Rosenberg, M.D. Their studies showed that exercise provided significant improvements in 70-, 80-, and 90-year olds' abilities.

Although Ben had been active all his life, it was hard even for him to believe exercise could make such a difference. Since he had played tennis for more than fifty years, Bob helped him recognize that advances in strength-training research were similar to those fancy titanium tennis rackets that have replaced the wooden ones Ben used to play with. "That was a good analogy, and it made perfect sense to me," Ben said. "But I didn't want to be some guinea pig somewhere that was just experimenting with new stuff. I was interested in a professional, quality, training site, with researchers."

Bob found the Ruby Gerontology Center at California State University at Fullerton (CSUF) had a state-of-the-art program. Ben and Bob wanted the support of Ben's doctor, who was actually more difficult to convince than Ben. "At first the doctor's attitude was, 'Hey . . . the guy's 100, he's obviously done something right—just let him be,'" Bob said. "And the doctor also felt this was simply natural progression for someone his age. Nothing could stop it, and it was a waste of time to try."

Ben felt differently. The research material convinced him that Bob was right. He was headed for a fall unless he improved his balance and mobility. And so the journey began. Twice a week Ben and Bob made the 100-mile round-trip trek to the Lifespan Wellness Clinic at CSUF, where they were introduced to co-directors Drs. Jessie Jones and Roberta Rikli. The primary mission of the Lifespan program and research is to prevent frailty in older adults through a unique program focusing on exercise, strength training, and mobility exercises.

"I was impressed with the philosophy and the program. And although I'd never worked out with weights before, I began to understand just how important strength is to one's balance and ability to get around. Being physically active is a major contributor to maintaining one's independence and quality of life," Ben said.

"One of the most important things Ben learned in this program was that he has some influence over his quality of life," Bob said. "He learned leg strength is key to his balance and independence. When the legs go because of declining muscle strength, it can start a domino effect. You don't get up and around as much, then the balance goes, which sets you up for a fall, and then it's just one problem after the next. When I lost fifty pounds, the majority of my back problems disappeared right along with the extra weight, and now I feel great. So we give credence to the fact that lifestyle changes definitely work!"

Ben and Bob also took up archery and competed in the local Senior Olympics. Since the sport requires accuracy, strength, and balance, the exercise routine paid off with a gold medal for Ben at age 101 and a silver for Bob at 55!

"I'm living proof exercise works, at any age!" Ben said. "And I think this is important, not just for the personal benefits, but also the economic value of personal responsibility for health, wellness and prevention. Our country is facing an expensive health care challenge, but we can help by taking better care of ourselves so we don't overuse the system. There's a lot we can do to combat the frailties and costs of aging, and people need to realize this and take action. Maybe we can save some Medicare dollars and increase a person's quality of life— that's a winning combination!"

Ben and Bob's incredible journey will continue as they experience life along the way. Ben says that considering the way he feels now, he's optimistic he'll be on this trail a while, at least until the next century, when he just may make history.

Vincent Malizia, 83

Northridge, California

I t's quite a responsibility to say you want to be a role model for others, but Vincent is ready for the challenge—in many ways, he has already succeeded. Not many retire at the age of 80; not many take up running at the age of 73, and even fewer still compete in their first marathon at the age of 80! This is Vincent's retirement lifestyle, and he says he's getting younger, not older.

"I don't feel old at all," Vincent claims. "In fact, I feel like my body's actually been rejuvenated by all the activity I have in my life. I'll never let my body get old—from the neck down I've probably got more muscle definition than most 30-year olds! I feel young too, and really can't believe I'm 83 myself!"

Vincent had no plans to be a runner. Out on one of his regular walks, he noticed a group of runners being coached by the famous former Hungarian Olympian Laszlo Tabori. Laszlo was the third man to break the four-minute mile record in 1955, after Roger Bannister accomplished it in 1954. Now he was at the track teaching people of all different levels how to run. "I couldn't pass up the opportunity to learn to run from one of the greatest runners ever, so I started working out with the group a couple of times a week."

Vincent remembers when he first started he couldn't even run around the block. He kept improving and before he knew it, he was ready to train for a marathon. "I chose the Los Angeles Marathon as my goal, and after seven rigorous months of training with coach Pat Connelly of the Roadrunners [a local running club] I was in the best shape of my life and ready to accomplish the task."

Vincent's desire to complete a marathon at the age of 80 is unique. Even though there are others his age, and even some older, who have run a marathon, there are very few (if any) who have accomplished it after taking up the sport as late in life as Vincent did. "I've been blessed with good health, but I have also helped God out a bit by taking care of myself. I've watched my diet by eating very little meat and lots of fresh fruits and vegetables. I keep busy by doing all my own home maintenance and yardwork, and I also have a good balance of activities. I love painting and art, attending church, and spending quality time with my family."

Vincent has been married to his wife Gina for fifty-six years, and they have two children and three grandchildren whom they absolutely cherish. Gina supports Vincent's running by attending every race—to greet him at the finish line. She also dishes out the daily vitamins. Vincent has no idea what they are, but his wife tells him they're good for him so he takes them.

"Aging is a funny thing," Vincent said. "It's really an attitude. I think you have to believe in yourself and not allow others to tell you you're old; otherwise, you might believe them. My running has contributed to how I feel about aging, because I have accomplished things I never would have dreamed I could do. This added self-esteem has provided me with the courage and confidence to take on just about anything—including age!"

Not only has Vincent amazed himself, he continues to amaze those around him. From the track pals he trains with to people he sees along his running route, it seems there are lots of people inspired by his accomplishments, cheering him on along the way—which he claims is a true source of motivation, too!

Fred Martin, 68

Long Beach, California

There are certain personality traits that seem to follow one throughout life. Some people never really change, but rather their daily world changes. That's what makes retirement a new adventure for so many, or perhaps it's a continuation of the world they didn't have much time for while they were working— now it's time for fun!

Fred has always been a "do-er," on the go, doing something or going somewhere. He's athletic and takes pride in his physical condition, whether during his high-school sports days, his twenty-eight years as a firefighter, or even now. Good health and doing make Fred tick.

Having been in great physical condition most of his life, Fred was surprised when he heard that he needed a five by-pass heart operation. Considering the stressful situations and amount of smoke inhalation he endured, he's been fairly fortunate, especially since he injured just about every part of his body during his time on the force.

It took Fred a year to return to the physical condition he was in before the operation, but during this time he engaged in some activities he may not have found again, if it hadn't been for the surgery. "I used to compete in table-tennis tournaments in high school and was even ranked number one—but then I got into martial arts to help quicken my hand speed and got my black belt instead. I still played table tennis off and on just for fun, but it wasn't until I was on a cruise recovering from the heart operation, that I started to get hooked again."

As it turned out, Fred has been back at competitive table tennis for the last several years. He's traveled to

tournaments and won numerous medals in various competitions, but he's also enjoying the side benefits, the camaraderie and social element of meeting neat people.
Additionally Fred is utilizing his crafty handyman skills
to help repair the "bats" (paddles) for some of the guys.
Overall he claims he's just having lots of good fun.

"I've played in the Fireman's Olympics, where I've
developed a reputation because some of the younger
guys groan when they learn the 'old man' is their oppo-
nent! They don't want to play me . . . I guess they fear
the wisdom!"

Fred thinks there's too much made about the aging
thing. "It doesn't matter how old you are . . . you have
to have goals. Maybe the goals are different as you get
older, but you have to strive to do better, or get better.
I've always pushed myself, not to the point of injury or
danger, but toward improvement. If one hundred sit-ups
is good . . . then I'll do a thousand! It's a personality
trait, and I apply it to all aspects of my life . . . always
have and probably always will."

Although Fred has transitioned nicely from the heart
surgery, a nagging knee condition from twenty-five
years ago required him to have a knee replacement.
While the doctors projected six months to get back to
normal and eight to ten months before he'd have
strength back, Fred did it in four months, because that's
just the way he does things.

Part of his phenomenal rehabilitation is due to his
workout regimen three days a week at the gym. Fred
starts with a thirty minute cardiovascular workout on
the treadmill or Stairmaster followed by a strength
workout with free weights and machines, and he concludes with swimming. He'll be the first to tell you that
this definitely contributed to his recovery from both the

181

heart and knee surgeries, as well as helping to keep his arthritis under control.

In addition to all of this, Fred also talks about the value of family and a loving wife. He's been married for forty-four years to Katie, whom he considers his best friend. "We firmly believe that one of the secrets to a long, happy marriage is being able to hum along without too many roller-coaster highs and lows," Katie said. "We still have fun and tease each other all the time . . . and we're still intimate, too, so why stop now? One of our favorite things is giving each other foot massages, and I love candles, too — but you know men, Fred always wonders what's burning!"

Some things never change with age . . . and it appears the secret here is to never let them.

Jane Mathis, 79, and Ida Via, 78

Dallas, Texas

You've heard the phrase "surprise attack," but who would think of using this phrase to describe the motivation behind a pair of seventy-something women interested in learning the art of Tae Kwon Do karate as a means of exercise and self-defense?

Both Ida and Jane are members of "The Steel Magnolias," a karate demonstration group from the Cooper Fitness Center which perform at various sites all over the Dallas area. Unusual, yes, but it has provided these women with improved health and a self-confidence level that both agree has "sky rocketed" since they joined the class.

"People don't often think of self-defense issues with age, but actually a small, dainty older woman can be a direct target for thieves and attackers," said Ida. "Those

crooks will be in for a big surprise if and when they attack me, because I know how to react and now don't worry as much as I used to about being a victim."

It was an attack on Ida that impelled her to take her first Tae Kwon Do class at the Cooper Center four years and four belts ago, too. Today, Ida is a blue belt studying for her brown, which consists of three tests—and then it's on to the black belt. But it's not the belts that keep her going . . . the real incentive is how she feels.

"I feel so much better physically, emotionally, mentally, and I've definitely noticed a big difference in my confidence level," Ida said. "Before, I always considered myself the 'nice little lady,' but now I speak right up and feel I'm more assertive in all areas of my life. I take control of situations now because I know I can—and I owe it all to Tae Kwon Do."

The physical improvements have also left an impression. Ida knows she sees the doctor less than before, and the exercise associated with this form of karate has improved her balance and strength too. "As people get older, we're more susceptible to falls and illnesses. The Tae Kwon Do emphasis on stretching, flexibility and range of motion improves circulation and overall health, as well as increasing strength and balance, which are key factors in preventing falls."

Ida has long believed in the benefits of exercise but strength-training was a new activity, so she worked with a personal trainer to determine what was best for her, and most importantly, how to do them correctly to avoid injuries. "I do this so I won't become bent over and unable to move around easily. I want to keep my good posture and my back strong and straight so I can keep moving and doing things."

For Jane Mathis, another member of the Steel Magnolias team, recognizing that she needed to take care of everything herself upon the death of her husband was her motivation to get involved in the exercise group. The course called "Self-Defense for Women of Small Stature" intrigued her . . . little did she know it was karate, but since she was alone, Jane needed to be able to protect herself.

"On my first day, I asked the instructor if this type of activity would be too strenuous for someone like me, and he suggested I observe the class to determine if it was right for me," Jane said. "And that very day, I spotted an old friend in the class, and when she told me how much she enjoyed it . . . I knew I could do it, too!" Jane has experienced benefits that are beyond just physical. She's made new friends in the process, too. "This a great group of people who genuinely care about each other. Plus, we've actually formed an extra-special bond because others think we're all a bit crazy to be doing this!"

Jane has continued in Tae Kwon Do for the past three years and strongly encourages others to try it. "So many people are concerned with stopping or slowing the aging process. I know the improvements I've experienced have slowed it down for me, and I can feel the difference when I miss a class if other appointments come up . . . I feel sluggish, have low energy, and know I better get back quick before problems start setting in!"

The Steel Magnolias demonstrations are what Ida and Jane enjoy most. By showcasing their skills and talking with the audience, they often change people's mindset about what's possible with age. Sometimes, they admit, they feel like "oddities," since so much emphasis is put on their uniqueness and age, but they still strive to inspire others to enjoy the variety of benefits they've discovered.

June McClean, 83

Visalia, California

She's known around town as the "Groovy Granny," a nickname from her grandson, who introduced June for "Show & Tell Day" at school and called her "groovy." Today, June is nationally recognized as the "Groovy Granny" due to her vivacious outlook on life and activities that defy the aging process. From teaching aerobics to an 80th birthday skydive, June loves life, and her enthusiasm and vitality make her an inspiration to most everyone she meets.

She's figured out a way to age without getting old. It's called exercise, and for those who think it's too late to make a difference, think again—or take a look at June, who's been teaching aerobics for the past twelve years and has a fabulous figure and shapely legs to prove it. "Over-the-hill is a state of mind—my motto is never give up," June said. "You've got to have a lot of guts, as well as heart, and I do. I hope to be teaching until I'm 100!"

In addition to having a healthy heart, June also has a good heart. She's positive, motivating, encouraging, and genuinely committed to improving people's health. Her classes are always full, and if any of her students are sick, June always tries to visit them. In addition to her classes, she has written a book on fitness and nutrition for seniors, released an exercise video, and been featured in numerous newspaper and magazine articles, as well as on national television shows including *Oprah* and *Geraldo*.

June will admit she never expected to be doing this, but she learned long ago that things never turn out like you expect, so you've got to have faith. Being a cancer

survivor, June believes faith and a positive spirit were key to her recovery.

"When I came to America from Australia in 1934 at the age of 20, I planned to marry a tall, dark, handsome, rich American. Then I men John—a short, blond, wild Irishman who loved to drink and didn't have a dime to his name. However, he became quite successful after we married and for sixty-three years has made me the happiest gal alive. I really feel like I'm the luckiest person in the world to have found him."

June's fitness interest began in an effort to lose weight after the birth of her five children. Like many, June got hooked on exercise with Jack LaLanne on TV, and now she serves with him on the Governor's Council on Physical Fitness and Sports. "I was thrilled and honored to be appointed. Our missions are the same: to educate and enable people to live healthier lives through exercise, so I feel right at home with this group."

June is certainly comfortable in the spotlight. She posed for the Sensational Seniors Calendar, jumped out of a plane for her 80th birthday skydive adventure, and serves as a national spokesperson for Schwinn Cycling's new "Johnny G. Spinner." "It's the latest in fitness classes, and it's done wonders in strengthening my heart, lungs and legs—I feel like a million bucks! It's all done on stationary bikes, to music, with an instructor. I saw the young kids doing it and said why not? So I jumped on, gave it a spin and have been spinning ever since!"

June's always believed exercise should be enjoyable and fun so that it will be done regularly to receive its health benefits. It's evident this message has been well-received by those who attend her classes, because many of her "regulars" have been with her since she started teaching. "I wouldn't be doing what I'm doing if it weren't for my students and support from my husband, family and friends," June said. "Life is wonderful and being healthy is life! So when you love what you do, and have all the people you love around you . . . that makes live worth living!"

June's certainly made the best of her life and continues to do so. She has her share of challenges, but she maintains a positive disposition which she credits largely to her faith in God, and a belief that everything always works out for the best.

It's a groovy way to live.

Winfield "Win" McFadden, 93

San Diego, California

His nickname is more than just short for Winfield—it exemplifies his attitude about life. Win began a new life in retirement, and win he did. He won more than just athletic endeavors—he learned about winning at life. "A terrible thing has happened in our society. Too many people have self-defeating and sometimes self-pitying attitudes that confine them to a prison of ill health, want, and dependence on others," Win said. "The ironic part is that these attitudes contribute to the exact thing older adults don't want: to be in poor health and dependent on someone. Our later years can be a time of good health, joy, and independence. I'm living proof it can happen. I did it; I've seen others do it, and I want to help more people know they can do it too!" he said.

Win began his retirement by experiencing new adventures and activities not done since his youth. At the age of 63, he laced up his track shoes and started walking. One day, while enjoying his new morning ritual, he heard that the first-ever Masters track and field meet was going to be held in San Diego, and a 6.1-mile walk was one of the events. He knew he was by no means in top shape, but it sounded like fun, and since he was interested in exploring the world of track and field competition again, Win decided to give it a try.

"What the heck, I thought. I knew I could do the distance, maybe not real fast, but it was the masters division, which meant it was for the ages of 40+. Plus, I was curious and figured it would be something new to do. I ran track in high school and college but hadn't been to a meet since then, so going back after all that time would be an adventure in itself."

As it turned out, Win did compete. There were only seven other entries in his event, and even though he finished last, that was O.K. because he knew he hadn't trained enough anyway. He still had a great time and knew he could improve, which gave him the incentive and a goal to shoot for. It was the first step in a whirlwind of competitions, world records, travel, and literally hundreds and hundreds of trophies for Win. In fact, that first race in San Diego turned out to be the only event in the past thirty years where Win didn't win a medal!

Today, Win is a world-class senior track star. He has set thirty American and world records, including several while in his eighties and nineties. His events have included the long jump, triple jump, high jump, javelin, discus, 100- and 200-meter dashes, and the racewalk. *Sports Illustrated* termed him "the Bruce Jenner of the seventy-and-over set," and the *Toronto Sun* called him "perhaps the finest 70-year old athlete in the world."

For Win, it's more than just winning that makes him go. "Getting out and having this activity to do has made a significant difference in my life. It's enabled me to be more life-oriented rather than age-oriented. I'm living each day doing something healthy for my body, which has not only made me feel better, I also don't feel old. Now I look forward to my birthdays because it puts me in an older race division!"

Today at the age of 93, nothing's changed—he's still at it. Although he's not traveling to meets like he once did, he's still competing, and for the last several years he's earned the honor of being the oldest competitor at a number of events. Currently Win is training for the next

Senior Olympics, where he plans to compete in the 1,500-meter walk and the discus.

Win's at it every day. After breakfast he goes down near the beach and does his "walk-out," and one day a week he'll practice on the track for speed and timing. But he also does other exercise activities. For twenty years he taught a senior exercise class at his church, which he still attends occasionally, and on Tuesdays he takes a line-dancing class that he even teaches one time a month!

Whatever activity people choose to do for exercise, Win believes fun is the operative word—otherwise people won't continue to do it, and then the problems associated with a sedentary, inactive lifestyle begin. "My wife Leota and I do a lot of ballroom dancing, which we absolutely love!" Win said. "In fact, a fair number of the trophies in our room are from our dance competitions. We don't compete anymore, but we did up until just a few years ago. We still try to go dance at least once a week."

Win and Leota share a beautiful relationship, having been married for sixty-seven years. Perhaps it's the re-sult of having their priorities in the right place, for they believe family always comes first and often say they come from a way of life where marriage is forever. Leota has been a tremendous source of support for Win, and he for her. Although Leota has suffered in recent years with a painful nerve disorder, she says that her work in help-ing coordinate Win's events, as well as exercising herself, have helped her cope by taking her mind off the constant pain of her condition. They go to church every Sunday, too, and are a true team in every sense of the word.

Win continues to rally others to join his team of healthy seniors by encouraging older adults to become physically fit and thus lead more healthy, joyful, and vigorous lives. He believes everyone has the chance to be healthier than they are, regardless of their age, and he is 100 percent committed to this effort. He even wrote a book about it when he was in his 80s entitled, *You Don't Have to Act Your Age*!

"One of my true passions is to share my experience with others and hopefully encourage them to win, too," Win said. "I think I've helped a lot of people look at aging differently, and if that's inspired some, then that's wonderful and I am happy!"

Win has certainly won at more than just athletics—he's helped people see what's possible with age. And that may just be the ultimate victory.

Ralph Merten, 88

San Marcos, California

Hanging inside the garage, above and in front of his new VW camper van, is an array of hats that one could call "trophies" representing numerous hiking adventures all over the world. Never would Ralph have believed that the very joy that kept him in tip-top shape, would also help save his life, but it did.

On his 87th birthday, Ralph was involved in a horrific, freak car accident that nearly took his life. Fortunately, thanks to a terrific medical team, quick-acting witnesses, and Ralph's remarkable physical condition, he survived. There was no way he could have avoided the wreck, nor did he ever see it coming. A heavy wrecking ball and cable had come loose from a truck traveling on the overpass above Ralph, and when he drove by, the cable suddenly pulled taut, spun his van around, and hurled Ralph straight up against the roof of the underpass. There were skidmarks from Ralph's van on the underside of the overpass. The van sat wedged for several minutes as passersby and firefighters tried to remove Ralph and also keep the van from rolling down the embankment.

"I don't remember any of it," Ralph said. "When I finally regained consciousness after two weeks in the hospital, I asked my son what had happened. As he showed me all the clippings from the newspapers, I couldn't believe it. If I hadn't seen it for myself—been involved in it myself—I never would have believed anyone would have survived. And when I saw the pictures of my VW van, I gasped and said, 'my car . . . oh no!!' To which my son replied, 'It's O.K., we'll get another one, Dad, but

next time you're getting a Hummer' (referring to the tank-like vehicles used in the military)!"

His body took a severe beating. He suffered twenty-eight fractures involving thirteen ribs, and a punctured lung made breathing almost impossible. Fifty percent of his lung capacity was gone, which meant he had to take quick, short breaths and be very careful not to get out of breath—which happened far too often for Ralph's liking. "The doctor told me 98 percent of people my age would have died with the type of injuries and trauma my body suffered," Ralph said. "And the reason I didn't was because my physical condition was probably better than most people half my age. I was in training for a lifetime dream trip to hike the Italian Alps, and although I didn't get to take the trip, that may have saved my life."

As a goal and inspiration in his rehabilitation, Ralph's hiking buddy, Jan, set a goal for them to hike down the Grand Canyon, and it worked. Faithfully, every day for ten months, Ralph did something physical to ready himself for that trip. "It was a long, slow process that started with me walking out to the mailbox. But after six weeks in the hospital, I was happy just to be moving." He did a variety of training to prepare for the Grand Canyon trip, including hikes on the six-hundred-foot Las Posas Mountain near his home.

"Each day on the trail, I would place a rock at the point I had made it to the day before, and then the next day I would try and go a little bit further. My goal concept worked again, and eventually I believed that I really could make that Grand Canyon trip. When we got there we learned that the oldest person on record to hike up and down it had been 86 years old. I was 88, and thus would be the oldest to ever do it. And I had additional incentive to make it: a mule ride out would cost

$750 and a helicopter would be $1,500—so I was committed to hike in and out . . . and I did! But hiking out took me eight hours, and I used to do it in six!"

Life changes, and Ralph understands when life throws a curveball, you need to figure out how to hit it. When his wife was diagnosed with and eventually died of Alzheimer's disease, Ralph was there for her, taking her on a new adventure every day, exploring new things, and giving her support. He's very familiar with the value of family and friends and knows the important role they played throughout his own rehabilitation. For that, he says, he will be eternally grateful.

He also obviously believes in the importance of goals. Although Ralph will continually struggle with the changes in his life, he will cope, because he has things he wants to do in life . . . and he plans on doing them.

"Hiking has enabled and inspired me to survive, and given me the incentive to reach my goal of enjoying more adventures yet to come. Perhaps I'll top my own record as the oldest hiker in and out of the Grand Canyon and do it at the age of 90!"

Mike Moldeven, 80

Del Mar, California

One of the benefits of growing older is the wisdom one attains from experience and the opportunity to pass these lessons on to future generations. Wisdom is shared through communication, which can bridge generation gaps and create special relationships between grandparents and grandchildren. These special relationships are often cherished throughout a lifetime.

"I've had a long, continuing interest in intergenerational communications," Mike said. "Of course, that comes from being a grandpa! I also believe these relationships are healthy and essential to both grandparents and grandchildren, and I'm committed to helping people get them established."

Mike has written books and articles—some of which have appeared on the Internet—to help grandparents interested in learning how to connect with their grandkids. "There are so many barriers today separating grandchildren from their grandparents—whether it's distance or circumstance. We need to help people eliminate these barriers and get them interacting again!"

Distance was the barrier separating Mike from his grandchildren, so he spent a lot of time writing them letters, sharing fun stories from his past as well as various other family anecdotes. After awhile the letters started piling up, and his grandchildren suggested he make them into a book—so he did.

"The first one was titled *Write Stories to Me, Grandpa*, followed by another one titled *Grandpa's Notebook*. I self-published them and sold more than two thousand copies of each. What people really wanted to know, was how to get started establishing communication with grandchildren. So I created a newsletter for grandparents filled with information and ideas to help them, but now I refer people to articles on the Internet through America On Line's SeniorNet and the AARP forums."

Establishing intergenerational relationships is an important element in maintaining family legacies and sharing the values and traditions of the family and society. With grandchildren, particularly, one of the best ways to communicate is often through family stories. An additional benefit is that this interaction helps establish a meaningful relationship between grandchildren and grandparents.

"If grandparents are not there to communicate and interact with their grandchildren, kids lose perspective on what it means to grow older. They miss out on that special relationship and the opportunity to be loved by older family members beyond just Mom and Dad. It's so important to have these relationships—to be able to share life with each other."

As important as these relationships are for grandchildren, they are equally beneficial for grandparents. They establish a sense of continuity and an opportunity to pass values on to future generations. "Grandparents are terrific storytellers! Oftentimes they are the only ones who can share these family stories that carry the traditions, culture, and history on to future generations," Mike said. "Plus, it can provide them with a sense of meaningfulness and connection within the family which can greatly contribute to their desire to live and passion for life!"

Mike vividly remembers the difficulty he had dealing with the loss of his wife, Gail, and he believes the strong support from his family was key in his ability to cope and continue on with life. He recognizes that overcoming loss and changes that can come with age can be a challenge, but he also knows that connecting with others, whether they are family or friends, is essential.

"Life is worth living when you are contributing to it. I know I'm proud of my age and consider it to be quite an accomplishment! I'm thrilled I've made it this far . . . and I plan to do a lot more living, too, because there's lots of sharing still to be done. To me, that's life! In fact, the way I see it is very positive—if you're lucky, you get to be old! And that means getting to share."

Bert Morrow, 85

San Marcos, California

Some things never change with age. Maintaining a healthy diet and exercising regularly have proven to be important for all ages. Keeping mentally fit also plays a role, as does keeping oneself challenged. Yet the challenges 85-year-old Bert Morrow discusses make you forget all about age. Maybe that's the real secret of aging well: not thinking about your age, just do it!

To say things get better with age is an understatement for this athletic gent who didn't even start competing until the young age of 69. Since that time, Bert has been the recipient of more than 29 world championship medals and 115 medals from the U.S. National Championships. His first Masters world record was at age 76 in the 80-meter hurdles, and recently Bert set three new American and world-records for the 60-meter sprint, 60-meter hurdles and the 200-meter sprint at the National Indoor Track and Field Championships in Boston. His athletic accomplishments also landed him the star role in an award-winning national television commercial for Chiquita bananas.

His diet is one Euell Gibbons would have been proud of, since it consists mainly of fruits, grains, and vegetables. His breakfast begins the night before when he soaks a mixture of thirteen raw grains and seeds overnight. In the morning he drains off the liquid and tops the combo with honey, banana, and bee pollen. His liquid refreshment is equally intriguing, the "aloe vera cocktail," with a squeeze of lime or a twist of lemon added to this juice-and-water concoction that Bert's been drinking for more than twenty-five years. He was apparently ahead of his time with this concept, because aloe vera juice is now being touted for its exceptional antioxidant powers.

Exercises start off the day, with his first stretches being done in bed. Then it's on to the "Gravity Gizmo," as Bert describes it, a contraption he straps himself into and hangs upside down while performing sixty inverted sit-ups, bringing his hands up to touch his toes. Following this ritual, the day continues with more stretching on the floor, totaling thirty minutes in all. It's a routine he swears by and says nothing ever gets in the way of!

"I don't think people have any idea how important flexibility and stretching are to being able to move, prevent falls, and just plain get around," said Bert. "And it's particularly important as one gets older, since it's generally pain and stiffness people complain about and blame on old age—in many cases it's simply not enough movement that is the real problem."

Bert believes movement is key to rejuvenating the cells in the body and staying healthy. He remembers reading about it in a book once, and he personally experienced the phenomenon several years ago when he retired and had a 53-foot ketch built so that he and his wife could see the world.

"We sailed 19,000 miles in three years. We were in the best shape of our lives when we returned because of the constant moving on the boat. Even when you're sleeping in your bunk, the ocean motion is continually moving your body, rejuvenating those cells, and making you feel great. I'm convinced there is definitely something beneficial about movement!"

Getting enough movement has become a daily priority for Bert. His weekly regimen includes two days of track work for speed and hurdles, and three days at a local university gym for his hour strength-training workout, which he also credits to improving his speed on the track. In fact, Bert improved his hurdle time from last year in a recent track and field competition—so those who think that one can't improve with age better check again!

"We do need to think differently about what's possible with age because mental elements play a key role," Bert said. "I credit my never give up mindset to something my grandfather said: "The difficult is easy; the impossible just takes a little bit longer." Bert believes nothing is impossible if you try and he gives new meaning to the saying, "some things never change with age!"

Mary Murphy, 79

Los Alamitos, California

Age has never been an issue in Mary's life, so why should it be now? She learned how to water-ski when most people are giving it up. In fact, she discovered a new way to water-ski that may encourage others to try it in their later years, too!

Mary celebrated her 79th birthday in an unusual and spectacular fashion: a little twenty-six-mile jaunt to Santa Catalina Island at twenty-two knots per hour, across the choppy Pacific, without stopping or falling—all on her waterskiing Air Chair.

"For my 50th birthday I did this same trip standing, but the Air Chair is the way to go now!" Mary said. "I started riding it about four years ago, and now I'm learning how to 'catch some air' by jumping the waves and taking it airborne, too!"

Co-invented by one of her sons, the Air Chair sits on a hydrofoil that rises three feet above the water when pulled by a ski boat. A wing-shaped aluminum blade attached to the base of the hydrofoil slices through the water just like a ginsu knife. All this attaches to the chair, simulating a ski . . . and off Mary goes.

As most waterskiing enthusiasts will tell you, this sport requires tremendous balance, finesse, and strength. Unfortunately these are not traits one would typically expect to have an abundance of with age, yet Mary shows it's possible with some effort, to have these skills—regardless of age.

"A couple of years ago, my son suggested I start going to the gym to build up my strength and make it easier to continue waterskiing. It was hard at first since I

really hadn't been to a gym since I was younger. It worked though, because it takes a lot of strength to hold on to that towrope for twenty-six miles to Catalina Island , especially at my age . . . but I can do it! And I have every intention of continuing these workouts because for my 80th birthday I plan to ski there and back again!"

Mary has taken good care of herself for years. In addition to her daily exercise, she is very careful with her diet, too. "Eating right plays an important role in our health as we grow older, " she said. "I'm also adamant about vitamins. I start every morning with a tablespoon of emulsified mint-flavored cod-liver oil, then with my lunch I take magnesium, zinc, calcium, and a good multivitamin . . . all to keep my bones strong and my body healthy."

But staying healthy with age is generally the result of a combination of things and Mary's vitality is undoubtedly linked to her positive mental attitude. " I don't mind telling people how old I am because I'm proud of my age. Too often people are so convinced they can't do something just because of their age, and then they never get the chance to surprise themselves. If you spend too much time thinking about what you can't do, you put an end to life. I never think of what may go wrong . . . I just get out there and do it!"

George Nissen, 83

La Jolla, California

I t's all a matter of balance—literally—according to George Nissen, who speaks from experience on the role exercise has played in his life. As the original inventor of the trampoline, and a gymnast extraordinare, George's trademark today is his famous handstand. He started perfecting this feat at the young age of 65, because it incorporates his belief in balance.

Excelling in these activities has become his way of life. He was the national tumbling champion in 1935, 1936, and 1937, and an All-American diver in 1937, too. George has given more than 2,000 trampoline, tumbling and gymnastic demonstrations to people of all ages around the world. Every year the Nissen Award is presented by the NCAA to the outstanding male collegiate gymnast in the nation. Similar in stature to the Davis Cup for tennis, the Nissen Cup, now in its 39th year, is recognized as the oldest annual international competition in trampolining.

His passion for the sport and his entrepreneurial creativity have grown right along with George. At the young age of 70 he founded the Nissen Sports Academy, which develops new sports and fitness products and sponsors over 500 fitness and anti-drug programs in elementary, junior high, and high schools. He owns more than thirty-five sports and fitness patents, five of which he invented after the age of 70. Additionally, he's received numerous awards, including the prestigious Distinguished Service Award of the President's Council on Physical Fitness and Sports.

George's proudest feat is having the trampoline become a medal event at the Olympics 2000. "I've worked to make it an Olympic event for as long as I can remember. It was to be featured in the 1980 Moscow Olympics, but the U.S. boycott ended that dream. Yet even before that, I joked with people about seeing it as an Olympic sport in the next millennium, referring to the year 2000 as being so far away. Who would have known that this was exactly when it would happen."

The idea of the trampoline came to George in his youth, when he and his brother would go to the circus and watch the trapeze performers rebound from the net. It looked like fun, so George was hooked. In college, he used a version of his trampoline design at a YMCA camp to teach children how to tumble and dive, but it wasn't until he joined a diving team in Mexico that he actually discovered the name for his invention. *Trampoline* is Spanish for "diving board," and since he was the All-American diving champion, his Mexico teammates called George the *campeon de trampolin*. The word just seemed to fit and has stuck ever since.

"It's all in the name of fun," George said. "If you can make an activity fun, then people will want to do it. That really became my mission." And it's a mission George continues to pursue today by demonstrating his own gymnastics abilities with his famous handstand. It's called a "press" handstand (performed from a push-up position to a vertical stand). He doesn't know of anyone else who can still do it at his age. Of course, George thinks it's fun and others agree—it always brings a smile to anyone within view.

Recently George wondered if he would ever be able to do his handstand again after a fall from a ladder. "At my age, the doctor was amazed I hadn't broken any

bones. When he looked closely at the x-rays, he was astonished by how strong my bones actually were and credited my exercise regimen. He also told me I probably would not be doing my handstands again anytime soon, but he was wrong, because here I am doing it."

Doing handstands takes a fair amount of strength, and being able to still do what he does at his age, after the fall, makes this ability even more incredible. George believes that much of his rehabilitation and good health is the result of a state of balance in the body and the mind. When things get out of balance in your life, that's when you're vulnerable and likely to get sick. "People forget about the importance of creativity and working to continually challenge the mind as much as the body. Then there are others who forget to challenge the body and only focus on the mind. This is why I talk so much about balance, because I believe you need both the physical and mental components working together, in order to live a long, healthy life."

George will continue to keep his body and mind in shape because he thinks it's possible he may have another twenty years or so to go and staying in balance may be the key to that reality.

Joe Norris, 90

San Diego, California

Joe's having a ball in retirement and he admits that he's having more fun now than he ever had working! He continues to play the sport he loves and today Joe holds the record as the oldest man in history to bowl a 300 game—at the age of 86! In fact, he accomplished this feat twice: the first time was in 1994, but he was not honored because it was a nonsanctioned event. No problem—he just did it again later that same year and officially received the designation.

"There's something about being involved with an activity, sport, profession, or whatever it is that you really love and staying involved with it throughout your whole life that I think makes you feel ageless," Joe said. "The amazing thing is, I feel like a kid. I've never felt old, ever. I have friends who look and act old, so I guess I'm just lucky in that respect . . . but it is a weird feeling!"

Joe spends a lot of time organizing bowling leagues across the country so that other seniors can experience the benefits of the sport. He has been elected to seven halls of fame, including the National Bowling Hall of Fame and Museum in St. Louis, better known as the A.B.C. Hall of Fame. He's also proud of his participation in the Senior Olympics competition, where he has won nineteen gold medals and nine silver medals . . . all by being part of something fun.

"I love life, bowling, and people . . . and not in any specific order, but I do believe I've been blessed by having these priorities in my life. I enjoy good health, have strong family roots, and never take naps—so when I go to bed, I really sleep! I've been active all my life and don't have much time for television. I'd rather read."

Yet Joe has also had to overcome a few challenges along the way: he had triple-bypass surgery and now reads every food label before he puts anything into his mouth. The most devastating time in his life was the loss of his wife, Billie, after fifty-nine years of marriage. He was so distraught that he wouldn't go through with a funeral. Instead, several months later he organized a Billie Norris memorial tournament, a bowling fundraiser for San Diego Hospice. It was a huge success, and this event, as well as his bowling family, are what enabled him to get through his grief and a very difficult time in his life.

"Life is a funny thing sometimes," Joe said. "I could have sat around feeling sorry for myself many different times along the way, but that's just not my style. I'm not a quitter . . . never have been and never will be . . . and that makes a winner out of anyone!"

And there is little doubt, Joe is that indeed.

Jim O'Neil, 72

La Jolla, California

J im remembers how his kids were embarrassed by their Dad running down the street in skimpy running shorts and how his doctor warned him that it was simply unacceptable for someone Jim's age to do those types of physical activities. But times change and today Jim is recognized as one of the nation's best age-group runners in the 5K and 10K distances and will readily admit running probably saved his life.

"I started running in my early forties, which back then was considered odd," Jim said. "I even ran early in the morning so no one would see me and freak out! I was on a health mission and didn't care what anyone thought. I needed to change some bad habits, like my never-ending quest to find the perfect martini, which possibly would have killed me in the long run . . . so run was what I did. The drinking stopped when the running started, and really, most everything else in my life changed, too. The people I hung out with, my activities, my health—and it was definitely all for the better."

Jim vividly remembers an indoor track meet featuring master runners over the age of 40, as an inspiring turning point in his life. He began by running around the block, and within a month he could run a mile. As it turned out, his first competition was also the first U.S. Masters Championships, and today, Jim is the only one who has run in all thirty of these events. He believes this record will serve as his motivation to continue competing.

"It used to be that sports stopped after college—part of that was attributed to the fact that doctors didn't approve of older people engaging in physical activities, certainly not competitively. There were no organized groups coordinating sports activities for older adults, so it just didn't happen. Today however, there are numerous opportunities for people to stay engaged in physical activity because we now know just how important it really is, both physically and mentally."

Attitude, Jim believes, has a lot to do with the aging process, too. "If anything, I feel younger than I ever did before. Not that defying the aging process was ever my intention, because that makes it seem like aging's a struggle . . . rather, I think it's an attitude that results in behaviors that ultimately make you feel better . . . and that was what I was after."

Jim is doing it right because he has established a slew of running records and is considered by many to be a legend in his own right. "Sometimes at races, people will come up and tell me that I've inspired them, and although I'm flattered, I'm also a bit embarrassed. They are the ones who inspire me—going out there and grinding it out in the middle of the pack, never expecting to win, but they're out there doing it, giving it their all . . . now that's great! So if I've contributed in any way to that, I am proud."

Jim is also proud of his children and seventeen grandchildren! He says he needs to run to keep his energy at the level required to play with them and do the things they love to do, like skiing and playing tennis. In fact, he says he does more now than he ever did at the age of 42! "Today, at 72, I run six miles a day and it's no big deal anymore. I've met lots of incredible older adult athletes, many who didn't start until their fifties, sixties, and even seventies. We all feel terrific and are living proof that it's never too late!"

Jim encourages others to give exercise a try, but he believes the real motivation comes when people start to feel better and have more energy. He warns beginners not to expect miracles overnight and to recognize that it took time to break the body down so it will take time to build it up, too—anything worthwhile takes time.

As one grows older, time is often the very thing people begin to fear the most, but in Jim's case and in the lives of many other master athletes, time is now working in their favor. As a result, there's a lot more living to be doing!

Jewett Pattee, 75

Long Beach, California

"Just do it" is his motto. Although he didn't coin the phrase, he speaks from experience, because physically he couldn't do much of anything before the age of 50, and he has the medical bills to prove it. "We can do a lot more than we think we can is what I've learned," Jewett said. "And believe me, if I can do it, so can others, because I couldn't even see my toes on account of my belly being so big. I decided to make a change, and if I hadn't, I wouldn't be here telling this story."

And Jewett has quite a story to tell. Today he is the only cyclist over 70 to ever complete three Race Across America (RAAM) events, billed as "the ultimate test of human endurance." The race starts in Irvine, California and finishes in Savannah, Georgia, covering 2,904 miles, over demanding terrain, in five to eight days, with a team of four riding between 350 and 530 miles a day. Jewett was a member of the first Masters team (60-plus age group) to ever complete the grueling event, which they did in a mere eight days, five hours, and seventeen minutes. This year Jewett hopes to break that record with his new team of riders, all age 70-plus.

"I'm proud to say I'm the oldest one who has ever done this race three times, especially considering I couldn't even get on a bike twenty years ago. I felt like I was already an old man back then—I was fat and inactive, had high blood pressure, borderline diabetes, arthritis of the spine, I smoked cigarettes, and was an alcoholic. Basically I was staring at the finish line of life, if you know what I mean. Having overcome all that and

participating in this event, I think I've earned the status of being one of the toughest guys alive!"

Certainly Jewett has come a long way since then. His life of self-destruction and illness has become a new life of health, positive attitude, daring challenges, and fitness. As a result, he no longer needs blood-pressure pills, his weight dropped, the symptoms of diabetes and arthritis disappeared, and he says he's never felt better.

"It all began with a single step, literally," Jewett said. "My first goal was to run one mile, and it took me a while to accomplish that, but I did and it felt good. Then I looked at my diet and changed it, too. As I kept setting new goals for myself, I realized I was really making progress."

Within a few years Jewett won a bronze medal in the 5K race at the local Senior Olympics competition, which led him to begin running longer and longer distances. Before long he was tackling marathons! But a couple of hip replacements made him switch to bicycling—and he hasn't stopped pedaling since. "Cycling's a lot easier on your body, that's for sure. I was able to run four marathons on my first hip replacement, but now that I've switched to biking, I think this second hip will last a lot longer—so far it sure has," he said.

Jewett took time recuperating from his hip surgeries, using an Exercycle initially and then challenging himself on the mountains of Oregon and California. By his mid-sixties he was competing in 200-mile cross-country races, and at age 70, he and his wife, Dorothea, rode a tandem bike, leading a group in a 1,750-mile ride from Canada to the Mexican border. "We can do more than we think we can—I surprised myself by accomplishing some of the things I have," Jewett said. "But good health is a challenge!"

Jewett also suffered with Meniere's disease, a virus that strikes the middle ear and affects one's hearing and balance. Although he lost most of the hearing in his right ear, the real struggle was just walking from the bedroom to the kitchen. He learned a lot about the importance of never giving up. "It's like vertigo, you can't even walk a straight line, let alone any distance. But I just kept pushing myself, refusing to give up. If I fell, oh, well—I'd just get back up. I wasn't going to let it beat me and I guess that's how I've approached all these challenges in my life after 50—I wanted to win."

Jewett believes it's important to be realistic with goals, otherwise people may end up in worse shape than before they started. If the goal's too high and unattainable, then they may give up entirely and feel like they have failed. Therefore it's essential to be practical before beginning any new endeavors. He also suggests having a complete physical before embarking on any new exercise regimen.

"Most all the people I compete with are older, so inevitably the majority have had some health problems to overcome," Jewett said. "The team I'm training with now for the upcoming RAAM event are all in their seventies and interestingly enough, two are ex-cardiac patients. We met at SCOR, the Specialized Coronary Out-Patient Rehab group, which started about twenty-five years ago and has now become an active cycling club. I've handpicked this team and I believe we're among the best long-distance riders around. I hope we'll break the course record . . . in fact, we may even beat some of the younger teams as well!" he laughed.

Jewett believes that because he and his teammates have overcome adversity, they are able to push themselves a bit harder than others. They know they can do it—they've been there before, in a sense. They know the difference between being unhealthy and feeling rejuvenated. "I don't ever want to be like I was when I was younger! There's no question things can get better with age—you just have to make a choice and then work at it. This is no different."

And work Jewett does, both on the bike and in the weight room for overall strength, toning, and conditioning. He also works on his diet, which he believes is just as important as exercise. The first change he made was to eliminate fat. While he knows the body needs some, he says it's almost impossible to eat zero fat with the average American diet. "My body seems to run best on a high-carbohydrate diet with lots of fresh fruits and vegetables. I found that I needed more protein in my diet due to my exercise, because the body burns glycogen and fat but it also burns muscle, and protein helps to replace that. So I eat more cottage cheese, chicken, maybe a little turkey for a change of pace—but virtually no red meat at all. The key is to keep it balanced, and if I have any snacks, I always make them healthy."

Additionally, Jewett takes antioxidants, which he considers vital and particularly important for aging athletes. Vitamin E, vitamin C, beta-carotene and selenium are on his list, and although he claims to be a bit of a nut about them—they work!

Balance is as key to cycling, as it is in the rest of Jewett's life. He and Dorothea will be celebrating their fiftieth wedding anniversary this year. They are thankful to have a wonderful family of four children, ten grandchildren (one who wants to be a cyclist when he grows up), and even a great-grandchild to share their lives with.

"What I had previously feared as a time of illness and idleness has become the most healthy, exciting and best time of my life. There are so many stereotypes that I think really hold a lot of people back. Some are afraid to try something new because they think they're too old to do it . . . but I say, who says? It's hard to overcome these beliefs, but you've just got to . . . too many quit too easily. I did what I thought was right, and it certainly worked for me!"

It's obvious that Jewett's drive comes from deep down inside, and he's definitely enjoying the ride of his life.

Annette Patterson, 67

Encinitas, California

Dancing has been her salvation. It brought her joy as a child, helped her heal from the loss of her spouse, and today it helps keep her healthy, feeling youthful, and always makes her smile. "I think I was born to dance . . . but I'm sure my grandmother, Nanny, influenced me because she loved to dance too, and I spent every summer with her," Annette recalled. "I remember going to the big dances every week with Nanny, and watching all the dancers in total awe. When I first learned how to swing, I tied a towel to a doorknob and that became my partner!"

Nanny was an inspiration, as well as a mentor to Annette. She was the only real source of happiness in Annette's youth. As a result, Annette is both thankful for the special relationship they shared and is sure that she molded much of her life after Nanny's because she sees a number of similarities.

"Nanny was always full of life, independent, and even bit of a rebel. She never depended on anyone, was as strong as a horse, drank, and ate pickled pig's feet. Amazingly, even after doing everything we know you're not supposed to (except smoke), she lived a long, healthy life and died at the age of 97. She made me laugh, she made me smile, but most importantly, she taught me how to love dance."

Annette found someone else who shared her love of dance: her husband of forty-four years, Wesley, who died of cancer a few years ago. They had a wonderful marriage, and even though it was cut short, she has treasured memories that will never fade.

"Sometimes I feel cheated, because I think the doctors could have done more. But I also know that we made the absolute best we could of the remaining time we had. I cared for him at home and made sure we did all the things he wanted to do . . . traveled, got a motorhome, a boat, just celebrated life!" When he died, Annette said her life turned to hell. "You can never prepare yourself for the impact of that type of loss . . . it's devastating. Everything you do, everywhere you go, reminds you of that loss."

Annette started fresh by selling her home, moving to a new town, and occupying herself with work and volunteerism. "I went nuts sitting around the house with little to do but think. I had to get out and get busy, which really helped keep my mind off of him." Dancing, however, was still the constant in her life, and although it was difficult to go it alone, she knew she just had to.

"Dancing swing is definitely my thing. It makes me smile, so it has to be part of my life. But it was hard to find partners who were compatible and fun, until one day, a man I'd been dancing with introduced me to someone he said was more likely my speed." But there was one problem—he was younger than she. There may have been a difference in age, but you'd never know it because Annette's in great shape and has never considered herself old. "I've always thought you're as old as you feel . . . and I don't feel old. In fact, when I say how old I am . . . it even shocks me. And when I look in the mirror, I don't think I look old and I certainly don't think old . . . so maybe that's the difference."

While there's no question dancing keeps her happy and in shape, the real secret may be her workouts. "Before I started exercising with weights, my muscles felt like they were turning into marshmallows—and in order to keep dancing, I knew I had to do something."

Annette enrolled at the local YMCA and began a routine to increase her strength and build the muscle back up in her body. She noticed improvement within only three weeks, continues to enjoy it and has no plans to stop. "I have more energy now and just really feel great. If I had known it would feel like this, I would have done this a lot sooner."

Dance will continue to be part of her life, to help Annette grow, heal, love and live life. And just as it has in all the days past, this seems like a smile that will certainly last.

Bert Powell, 76

Winter Park, Florida

T here is a certain discipline factor that comes with serving in the military, and there's little doubt this experience influenced Bert's retirement. With a belief that he "never really retired . . . except from the military," Bert has continued challenging himself physically and mentally. From his financial consulting, volunteer work, poetry writing, painting, and thirty years of serving as a clinical hypnotist (which included lectures to college psychology classes), it is his later life accomplishments in Tae Kwon Do which are most amazing.

Two weeks before his 69th birthday, a friend invited Bert to his first Tae Kwon Do demonstration. Impressed with the physical abilities of these martial arts presenters, he remembers feeling he would never be able to do those same moves, especially at his age. But his life experiences had taught him "never say never," and perhaps one of his favorite sayings—"If you think you can or think you can't . . . you're right!"—was the primary motivation for his signing up for the thirty-month black-belt program. "I never do anything halfway," said Bert. "It's always all or nothing with me, and I was prepared to accomplish this new challenge, just like all the others."

And he did, becoming a first-degree black belt at the age of 70, within only eighteen months. Today Bert is a fourth-degree black belt and believes so strongly in the benefits of this martial arts practice that he has become an instructor as well. The improved health he has experienced with his involvement in Tae Kwon Do motivated him to share these benefits with other seniors, too, so now he conducts classes at the local senior center.

"I want to entice more seniors to start Tae Kwon Do as a means of improving their health and living longer. It's so important to keep the body moving as we get older, but Tae Kwon Do also incorporates relaxation and meditation techniques that are equally beneficial."

Bert recognizes life changes with age, but he also believes in fighting back by learning ways to cope with these inevitable changes so they don't end up taking over your life. "You have to be strong mentally, physically, and emotionally to get through some of the changes that come with age. For example, when my wife died it was a difficult personal loss, but I also knew I had to keep going, to refocus my energy and attention in order to go forward with my life," Bert said.

Bert also suffered a heart attack a few years ago while performing at a Tae Kwon Do exhibition. His heart stopped in the ambulance and again for nearly two minutes at the hospital, but when he became conscious, he said he felt fine and was ready to go home. "Apparently, my performing the kicking demonstration triggered a dislodging of a build-up of cholesterol, which clogged one of my arteries and caused the heart attack," Bert said. "Fortunately, it didn't damage my heart muscle, so I was able to resume my regular activities relatively soon after the incident. The doctors also said that because I was in such good shape physically, the long-term damage was expected to be minimal."

Today Bert's healthier than ever and if you ask his opinion about how to age well, he'll tell you happiness is the primary influence on how people live their lives. "Finding happiness cannot be tied down to one location or thing. You should be able to find happiness anywhere. You can't buy happiness—you must work to accomplish it. You can't just sit around and expect happiness to come to you—you need to set goals and work to accomplish them. Then, you will feel good about yourself, which is key to finding true happiness that lasts . . . at any age."

Joe Raskin, 89

West Hills, California

Seeing seniors shuffle as they walked was something Joe observed far too often. So he created a senior exercise program at a local community center fifteen years ago—at the age of 75—and served as the primary instructor even though he is legally blind. "I can't read, but I can still see enough to get around. I know this is what people needed and I'm a do-gooder," Joe said. "If I can do something to help someone else, why not do it?"

With a background in physical fitness, Joe knows muscles, and he could see that too many seniors didn't have enough of them. He knew the right type of exercises could make a difference, help them feel better, have more energy, and maintain their independence longer.

"As people get older it seems they spend more time sitting, being sedentary," Joe said. "When that's done over a long period of time, the results can be catastrophic. Being stationary creates circulation problems, back problems, digestive problems—a host of different problems—even memory and mental aspects are affected. If blood isn't circulating, oxygen isn't getting to the brain and other parts of the body. There is definite truth to the saying 'Move it or lose it.'

Perhaps one of the biggest challenges Joe faced however, was helping people recognize that they could get better and feel better. Although the class was regularly full, there were still others who wondered whether it was really possible to improve with age, who believed that the "senior shuffle" was just the way it was, since many of them had been doing it for most of their later years.

"I don't know how we can convince people just how important exercise is. But I think it's imperative to re-educate people in their fifties and sixties that they're going to live a long time, and they need to recognize how important it is to take care of themselves. If you want to be independent, healthy, and active in your later years, exercise must be part of your plan. It's more than just eating right—you've got to move to keep on mov-ing!"

Joe thinks people spend more time worrying about getting older than doing what's necessary to make those later years a time of good health and vitality. He says he has no idea what old is and sees no benefit in spending much time thinking about it either. "I know I'm not old, and frankly I don't know if I'll even be old when I turn 100," Joe said. "Who cares how old you are . . . it's how you feel that should really matter—and as long as I'm still moving, I feel great!"

Paul Reese, 81

Auburn, California

There's a lot you can tell about a person by their shoes—where they've gone and where they're going, and Paul's been lots of places, this man and his running shoes. He's the oldest person to ever run across the USA, and much like the famous movie character Forrest Gump, once Paul had gone that far, he decided to run a little farther and be the first person to run across all fifty states. Some call it endurance running, but if you don't enjoy, you won't endure—so it's more than just about running . . . it's about life.

"I never thought I'd be running at this age; I thought I'd be dead!" laughed Paul. "I've already outlived both my parents by eight years, overcome cancer, battled with asthma, and even have spondylothesis (messed-up vertebrae). But I believe we make our own destiny, so I just keep on doing the best I can with what I have . . . and it seems to be working."

The idea to run across the United States came after reading a book about Don Shepherd, a South African who ran 3,200 miles across the continental United States in 1964. Paul was intrigued and wondered if he was capable of doing it. Although he had never been much of a distance runner, Paul began adding mileage to his regular three-mile stints and discovered he really enjoyed endurance runs. At the age of 54, he recorded a personal record marathon in a time of 2:39:28, almost a six-minute mile pace! After accomplishing that goal, he just kept on running—totaling twelve marathons, a 50-mile race and a 100-mile race, all within one year. Paul actually recorded his fastest times in his fifties and also became recognized as an outstanding age-class runner.

Once a Marine, always a Marine, and after a twenty-three-year career as a lieutenant colonel, discipline becomes a way of life. Discipline evolved into endurance running for Paul, which also involved goals, both setting them and working to achieve them. He believes it's more important than ever to have an agenda as you grow older—to have something to look forward to every day. He thinks too many people end up feeling old because they never develop an interest in something they're passionate about or have a plan for how to spend their later years.

"I'm sure longevity is affected by our genes, but in my case running has contributed to my abilities at this stage, particularly given my health and asthma. I'm not running so I can live long—it's the zest for life that running gives me—longevity is just a nice fringe benefit. I run because I feel better, eat better, think better, sleep better . . . do everything better! Ultimately, I do it because I enjoy it, and that's the only way to do anything."

It wasn't until after Paul retired from his second career as a school administrator, that he and his wife Elaine, set out to satisfy his long standing curiosity of running across the United States. "We packed up the motorhome and began our journey with a toe-dip in the Pacific Ocean north of San Francisco and ended with a splash in the Atlantic Ocean at Hilton Head, South Carolina. It was an incredible four-month adventure that covered twelve states, took seven pairs of running shoes, and totaled 3,192 miles . . . all at the age of 73!"

But that was just the first step. They enjoyed the experience so much they decided to continue on to the other thirty-eight states, which they did over the next four summers, with Elaine as the steady hand behind their temporary home on wheels and with two extra passengers—their Labrador retrievers. Once Paul ran across all the western states, they decided having gone this far, they might as well go a little further and finish the other twenty-two states east of the Mississippi, along with Alaska and Hawaii, too. Between the ages of 73 and 80 Paul ran a total of 23,288.5 miles!

Paul recognizes he's been blessed with good-enough health to accomplish this feat. However, three years before his trek across the USA he was diagnosed with prostate cancer. Although he endured some thirty-six radiation treatments, he was still able to get out and jog five miles each day of the treatment. His asthma has also been a continual challenge, and there were several times along the journey when he and Elaine thought he'd have to give up, but somehow he persevered. And when you add his vertebrae problem to all of this and realize that he always runs with a sacroiliac belt, the story becomes even more remarkable.

"It's all about thinking positively," Paul said, "and having incredible support from my family, especially Elaine. But I don't consider myself a 'superman' or anything—I just think we are capable of more than what we may think, and if you believe in yourself, it's simply amazing what you can accomplish."

In total, Paul has run 118,000 miles, and the joy of experiencing the journey with his wife and dogs, the only two labs he knows who get to take extended vacations, made it all the merrier! "The whole deal was wonderful, and it really brought Elaine and me closer, too, having this experience to share for the rest of our lives. She was my lifeblood, and I never could have done it without her. It wouldn't have been as much fun, and certainly part of the enjoyment was sharing it with her. She really was incredible to drive that motorhome some 60,000 miles, chasing after me! It will always be something we'll look back on and cherish."

So Paul continues on down the road, with hopes to run right into the next millennium: a man and his shoes, living and running with a real zest for life. And like Forrest Gump, who ran to get where he was going, not thinking it would ever take him anywhere, perhaps Paul's journey will take others places, too.

Paul's adventures have been chronicled in two books coauthored with Joe Henderson, West Coast Editor of *Runner's World: Ten Million Steps* (1993; story of the USA run) and *Go East Old Man* (1997; story of the adventures across twenty-two states west of the Mississippi)

Jhoon Rhee, 65

Mt. McLean, Virginia

T ae Kwon Do Grand Master Jhoon Rhee is actively recruiting members for his new "10021 Club" (pronounced one, double o, twenty-one), which stands for one hundred years of wisdom in the body of an 21-year old. From Jhoon Rhee's perspective this means living to the age of 100 and having the physical body of an 21-year old. Is it possible? With discipline, it just may be.

A world renowned 10th-degree black belt and considered the 'Father' of United States and former USSR Tae Kwon Do, Jhoon is one of the most elite martial arts experts in the world. He has been inducted into the Black Belt Hall of Fame, awarded the presidential "Daily Point of Light" honor and was the recipient of the martial arts "Man of the Century Award" along with Muhammed Ali for boxing and Joe DiMaggio for baseball. He is the author of numerous Tae Kwon Do books and has licensed studios all over the country bearing his name, including sixty in the U.S. and another sixty-five in the former Soviet Union.

If Jhoon's daily routine is any indication of what it takes to prevent age-related deterioration, he may already be on his way to having the physical make-up of a 21-year-old. He rises every morning at 5:45 A.M., drinks three to four glasses of water, and begins a three-hour workout: thirty minutes of meditation to music, then stretching, push-ups, and breathing exercises, including using a harmonica for his lung workout. His push-up routine is most extraordinary—he does a thousand a day, five hundred in the morning and five hundred in the evening!

Jhoon also follows a healthy, balanced diet, which includes a daily mixture of orange and cranberry juice, four or five bananas, and usually fish, raw vegetables, and lots of rice. He also admits he has a sweet tooth and needs more discipline to not eat cake, pie, or ice cream, but he figures he burns it off, so occasionally he will indulge.

For one to maintain this type of daily regimen, it's essential to have a strong mental mindset as well. "If people see me do this, then it's proof they can do it too," Jhoon said. "But they have to believe they can, and that is up to them. People can become whatever they think and do repeatedly: that's the power of the mind at work. Aging doesn't have to be a time of decline, but it seems too many people automatically turn a certain age and begin to think and believe it's natural to feel weak and tired—they let it happen. But it doesn't have to—I believe otherwise, and look at me!"

Jhoon obviously believes one's state of mind is caused not only by their internal thoughts but also by their actions, spoken words and chosen body posture or physiology. If emotions are triggered by actions as much as actions are motivated by emotions, there is a direct correlation between what we do and what we are or become.

In the seminars Jhoon currently conducts throughout the country, for a variety of people from corporate executives and senior citizens to members of Congress, he presents the seven life qualities of a champion and shows how these human elements are in direct correlation with the seven physical elements of Tae Kwon Do: 1) *Quickness* in kicking as the Tae Kwon Do element; *Alertness* in thinking as the human element; 2) *Endurance* in the martial arts; *Perseverance* as the human element; 3) *Timing* in kicking; *Punctuality* as the human element; 4) *Power* for punching is essential in Tae Kwon Do; *Knowl-*

edge as the human element; 5) *Balance* in Tae Kwon Do, to stand on one foot and kick with the other; *Rationality* as the human element balances the mind, soul and body, which equates to knowledge, honesty and strength; 6) *Flexibility* to kick without injury; *Gentleness* as the human element to be kind and understanding; 7) *Posture* in Tae Kwon Do shows the beauty of body movements; *Honesty* in the human element stands for character and shows the inner beauty of the person.

"These are the steps to success which incorporate the joy of discipline," Jhoon said. "And with these seven qualities as my foundation, combined with my life creed of knowledge in the mind, honesty in the heart and strength in the body, I have decided to live to 136, and believe I can do anything I set my mind to. I certainly don't plan to be the only member of my 10021 Club, so hopefully my leading by example will encourage others to join and follow in my footsteps."

Mildred J. Riley, 80

Los Angeles, California

"Joie de vivre!" is her motto. Some in her family call her a Pollyanna because she sees the world through rose-colored glasses and Mildred wonders what's wrong with that. She's happy, she's a survivor, and she continues to learn, grow, and experience new things. Isn't that what the joy of living is all about?

Mildred always believed things happen for a reason, but she certainly didn't expect to be a widow in her forties, or go through a divorce, or be a breast cancer survivor. She also didn't know that her childhood days of drawing on anything she could get her hands on were preparing her to become a computer artist in her seventies—as a means of healing. But sometimes that's just how things happen.

"Everything I do in life I do because I enjoy it," Mildred said. "I don't believe in giving up—what's the sense in that? If I didn't have my eyes, I'd still have my ears, and vice versa . . . I don't give in easily. I learn to cope with the cards I'm dealt." Of course, coping with widowhood at such a young age prepared Mildred early on to learn how to cope, and it was a valuable lesson because coping skills would be needed in the years ahead.

Anticipating her first grandchild, Mildred attended a doctor's appointment with her pregnant daughter and was asked when she had last had a mammogram. It hadn't been recently, so the test was set, and the next thing she knew, she was in the hospital for a biopsy. "The results showed such a tiny spot that I wasn't worried at all, being that I'm always so positive. As a pre caution, they wanted to perform the biopsy immediately, and I agreed it's always best to take the safe route."

Prior to the biopsy procedure, Mildred and her doctor discussed all the possible outcomes—if indeed the biopsy was positive and there was cancer, she felt it would be best to do whatever surgery was required, right then and there. "I trusted the doctor and saw no benefit in waking up to be told more surgery would be required later—why wait, was my attitude. I guess I must have known what I was doing, because that's ex- actly what happened—I had a mastectomy while in for a minor biopsy."

Mildred admits it was difficult for her emotionally, ac- cepting the new loss she now had to face. But she also knew that somehow she would get through it, because that's the way she's always been. "Every time I went for chemotherapy, which was a shot back then, I'd celebrate with a martini afterward, as my reward, and fortunately I never got sick!" Mildred laughed. "That lasted a year and a half—but I made it, and I'm still here to tell the story."

In addition to her chemotherapy, Mildred also saw a psychiatrist to help her deal with her emotional pain. She admits she was rather vain then, but dealing with a prosthesis was more difficult than she expected. "This isn't something to mess around with; breast cancer and a mastectomy are major emotional traumas, and anyone who doesn't think they are affected by it is kidding themselves. I'm generally positive and sure of myself, but after the surgery I had some self-doubt and these sessions really helped me deal with that."

Another important element in Mildred's healing was the psychiatrist's referral to an acupressurist. She'd never been to one before, but she did like trying new things so she agreed to go, with no idea where it would lead next. "Those sessions taught me how to let go and relax," Mildred said. "Of course, I didn't think I was up-tight, but he felt the tension in my body and encouraged me to get more involved in things I loved—that's how I initially got back into art."

Before long, Mildred was addicted to creating art. She couldn't get enough of it—up in the middle of the night, painting in the garage and ruining lovely nightgowns in the process. Sketching and painting in the car, getting paint all over, and never caring, because she was happy and having fun. "My art became part of my closure to cancer. It was like closing one door and opening another. It was a terrific feeling to be living again!"

Some of Mildred's favorite pieces were her creations made with items she got from the hospital during her surgery and follow-up treatments, including her old prosthesis. In fact, she made so many varieties that she eventually got sick of it and just quit making them one day. She knew then that she was finally done with that phase of her life. However, her love for art was back, she had rediscovered a joy in her life. "I learned computer art and loved it right away. It was scary at first because I didn't even know to type, let alone design art on a screen, but I overcame my fear by doing! Now I've got my own equipment—the latest in technology, and any-thing new that comes out—I've just got to have it!"

Art became a healthy healer for Mildred because it served as an outlet that has kept her engaged, chal-lenged, and excited. She also keeps happy and healthy by exercising regularly, feeling fulfilled, and being madly in love with her husband of twenty-one years, Chapin. Although she knows she's 80, she really can't believe it because she says she doesn't feel that old—and she certainly doesn't look it, either.

"I swore I'd never grow old gracefully . . . that I'd fight it every step of the way! But now that I'm here, I really can't believe it. I'm not old, and frankly, I don't think I ever will be because I enjoy life way too much to worry about age!"

Terry Robinson, 82

Los Angeles, California

"Come grow old with me . . . the best is yet to be" is one of his favorite quotes by the great poet Elizabeth Barrett Browning, and if you're looking for how this is done, there are few more inspiring than Terry. He's a living, breathing testament to the benefits of physical exercise over time. In fact, Terry's own physicians parade him around to other doctors to show them what's possible with age. It's a message Terry is also committed to sharing with others . . . the secret of vitality.

"It's about dignity and feeling good about yourself—and it's difficult to think right and feel right if you're not physically well," Terry said. "It has nothing to do with age; I'm 82 and feel great. I look at the body as a miracle, so I take care of it by staying healthy and fit."

Physical education and fitness are part of Terry's genetic makeup. He's been exercising for more than sixty years, much of it during a time when it was hardly fashionable. He was a personal trainer to the Hollywood stars and is in the Physical Fitness Hall of Fame. Today he still works out every morning and helps others benefit from exercise, too.

"We've come a long way . . . people are starting to understand just how critical exercise and movement are to our health," Terry stated. "The medical society is more aware of it, plus we've seen tremendous growth in the fitness field, particularly in the area of strength training and weight work. I've done it for years; I was always considered a nut, a 'musclehead,' but now more people know about the benefits, and frankly, I'm glad I'm alive to see this new awakening. It starts with our thinking, which effects how we feel about ourselves—if we don't feel good about us, then why bother with anything else?"

Terry is in terrific physical condition with a cheery disposition that's contagious. Serving as an example to others makes his message all the more powerful, so Terry spends a lot of time talking to older adults about

the benefits and importance of exercise—proving to them what's possible.

"I tell them to take a good look at me, then I tell them I'm 82. I think they're surprised to learn we're similar in age, but often look so different—that an 82-year-young body looks like me. The best news though, is that it's never too late to get better. We can build muscle in our seventies and eighties, and we need to in order to slow down the physical deterioration that's blamed on age."

From doctors to trainers to new clients at the gym, Terry is proof that exercise works. It's a lifetime commitment that obviously pays off. "If you look good on the outside, by being healthy and fit, think how good you look on the inside—the outside is a reflection of the inside. Exercise makes you feel better physically and it helps create a positive attitude—the ultimate key to life. If you feel good, you'll take care of yourself, inside and out, because you value yourself and your life."

Marilla Salisbury, 89

San Diego, California

Who would think that crossing a finish line would be the beginning of a whole new life? For Marilla Salisbury, that's exactly what happened, and it's a pace she's kept up for twenty years.

"Sunbonnet Sue," as she is often called because of the calico bonnet she wears when racing, has won more than four hundred national and international medals, received a plaque from President Reagan, and has been the spotlight of numerous newspaper, magazine, and television stories.

Marilla was never very interested in sports throughout her life, and she admits that she was always the last one chosen for any game in which one had to run. But things can change over time, and in Marilla's seventies she began competing in track and field events in exotic places such as New Zealand, Italy, Puerto Rico, Chile, China, Australia, and South Africa. "I used to be a sedentary lump," said Marilla. "I was crippled by osteoarthritis in my back, neck, and hips—so painful that I couldn't even tie my shoes. Talk about a pain in the neck: mine was so bad I nearly had to give up driving."

Yet it was while on a drive that she discovered a fitness center which ultimately put her on the right track. Motivating a 70-year-old who rarely exercised could be considered a daunting task. But when exercise was suggested as a way to help her feel better and manage her arthritis pain, Marilla decided to commit. It was the turning point in her life—the "medicine" she needed.

Marilla started slowly, spending most of two years working with weights to strengthen and limber up her body. She then graduated to running at the age of 72, and won a gold medal in her first 10K race! Concerned that running might aggravate spinal deterioration, Marilla's doctors recommended she take up walking instead, but she would not settle for just a typical leisurely stroll in the park. Racewalking intrigued her and she has since become world renowned for her speed walking at track and field events. Today she is a true inspiration to young and old alike.

Marilla leads a balanced life, recognizing the importance of physical, mental, and spiritual synchronization. "I believe my body is the temple of the Holy Spirit, and I have a sacred responsibility to take good care of it." Her husband Earl has been a tremendous source of motivation and encouragement, which Marilla credits as being invaluable in her success as an older athlete. Of course, believing in yourself is also key, as well as always striving to get better, whether it's physically or competitively . . . which evidently has little to do with age.

"I got my master's degree at 60, my tennies at 70, and now in my eighties I still feel great," said Marilla. "I must be doing something right because my doctor predicts I'll live to be 100!"

Kenneth R. Shaker, 81

San Diego, California

Not many people look forward to birthdays, particularly as they get older, but Ken doesn't mind—he already has his 82nd birthday celebration planned: an exhilarating parachute jump from an airplane at three thousand feet!

Ken has been jumping out of planes for years and doesn't see any reason to stop now, even if he is an octogenarian. Of course, these pleasure jumps he does today are a mere cakewalk compared to what he used to do. Ken was a World War II paratrooper who leaped into the night sky during the invasion of southern France during the Normandy invasion in 1944. He recently jumped again as part of the fiftieth anniversary commemoration of D-Day.

"There were forty-one of us from all over the world who returned for the fiftieth anniversary, and all of us did the jump in honor of that historical event," Ken said. "It was an interesting experience, jumping in front of an

Kenneth R. Shaker

audience of political officials, senators, dignitaries, and the Queen of England. It's a challenge, too, because you want to see if you still have what it takes to do it!"

Ken seems to like challenges. Whether it's debating with friends about foreign affairs or playing his regular weekly tennis match, he keeps himself involved in a variety of stimulating activities and credits this lifestyle to his longevity. "I never expected to be living this long. Since my Dad died at the young age of 46 from a heart attack, I just assumed I would go the same way."

In fact, Ken lived much of his life with the belief that he wouldn't be around long. This mindset began in his mid-thirties, when he would work for three years or so, then take three years off, then work for three years, and then not work. This pattern was influenced primarily by the early death of his father, and since Ken didn't expect to live long, this flexible schedule allowed him to enjoy life during his younger years, because he thought that would likely be all he'd have.

But he's still here. Maybe it's luck, or maybe it's because Ken took good care of himself as a safeguard against an early death. He's kept his mind sharp with lots of reading and believes most people know about the importance of following a good diet and getting the proper exercise, but a lack of discipline is what usually gets them into trouble.

"In the past, people didn't have to concentrate so much about getting the proper amount of exercise because the lifestyle was full of physical activity—working the land," Ken said. "But with all the modern conveniences today, we don't get as much exercise. Lots of older adults talk about low energy and tiring easily, but don't seem to realize that exercise can change that."

Ken agrees limitations come with age, so people need to accept the fact that the body may not move exactly like it used to—but it can still move, and that's what really counts. He's also a big advocate of the benefits of vitamin E, which he's been taking for more than thirty years. He says although there's no scientific proof of its benefits, he definitely believes it has been helpful for him.

"If I knew I would still be alive at the age of 81, I probably would have lived my life differently," Ken said. "But jumping from planes has worked for me this far, so I'm definitely keeping that 82nd birthday parachute jump reservation!

Virginia Shaver, 76

Anderson, Missouri

S he always wanted to go back to school and earn her college degree, preferably in communications. Virginia had long dreamed of becoming a writer, but she also dreamed of living a long happy life with her husband of fifty years. When he died of cancer and her life was turned upside down, she decided to make a positive change—so off to school she went. Enrolling at Missouri Southern State College, Virginia made history by becoming the oldest student on record—and the oldest dorm resident, too! It was an experience and the education of a lifetime—for everyone involved.

"I didn't know if my brain was going to be up to the challenge, especially having not been in school for more than fifty-two years," Virginia said, "but I'm happy to report that the old brain is the best computer in the world. Nothing compares; it worked like a champ! I wonder how many computers around today will still be current and functioning as well in fifty-two years!"

To save making a daily 75-mile round-trip commute, Virginia decided to move into a dorm on campus. "I became the resident grandma, literally, and encouraged the girls to visit anytime they wanted. I never felt like a misfit, I was one of the girls . . . just a little bit older! We had a great time—shared popcorn, stories and since I was the only one with a car, having wheels made me a really big hit!"

Virginia served as both a mentor and a friend. She talked with a homesick student until three in the morning, played matchmaker for another, and helped one write a paper on the Great Depression after the library closed. Faculty, friends and family were always there to support Virginia, too. When her health problems made school a challenge and almost forced her to quit, they all rallied behind her and encouraged her to finish.

Although Virginia's health made her feel like giving up, it also reminded her of how she felt when her husband died, and why she embarked on this endeavor in the first place. "When you go through the loss of a spouse, it's like part of your life has died too. You're so overwhelmed with emotion and feel like there is nothing that will ever help you heal. Friends try to help—but when it comes right down to it, it's a totally personal process."

Virginia remembers how a book entitled, *To Live Again*, by Genevieve Davis Ginsberg, who founded the Widow to Widow program helped her. "The secret is to

251

build a new life, to always keep yourself open to new things, and stay positive. At first this seems impossible, I know, because you don't want to build a new life, you want your old one back—but eventually you realize that's just not possible, and this is what you have to do to go on."

Virginia did complete her degree and graduated with the others. Her health is also coming back, and she's confident she'll achieve her goal of writing inspirational articles for religious magazines.

"You've got to feel good in order to want to do anything, but you've also got to do things in order to feel good!" Virginia said. "I've learned that I can do this. Even when challenges arise . . . I can overcome them if I just always continue to try." And that may very well just be the lesson for a lifetime.

Rosanne Shensa, 81

San Diego, California

C all it a coincidence or perhaps an intuitive sense of prevention—whatever it is, the Chinese approach their healthcare very differently than we do in the West. Never was this more apparent than when a Chinese doctor diagnosed Rosanne with a circulation problem one year before she suffered a heart attack, simply by feeling her pulse in various places on her body.

"In China," Rosanne said, "they seem to do a better job of prevention and treating chronic conditions, but the technology we have here is so advanced that we have the edge in more serious cases. Integrating the two philosophies, however, could be a real benefit to humanity and our healthcare system."

Rosanne has had her share of health challenges: two heart attacks, a broken hip, and a broken wrist. Yet she still describes herself as healthy. "Outside of an occasional heart attack . . . I'm in generally good health. Today I live my life by this simple rule: It's not how long I live, but how slow I die!"

Considering she learned from one of the longest-lived ethnic groups, Rosanne appears to be on the right path. She continues to share her knowledge by regularly conducting Qi (pronounced "chee") Gong exercise classes—something she's done for the past several years. "The gentle, slow movements of Qi Gong make it a good exercise for people of all ages, but particularly for older adults," Rosanne said. "Whether performed standing or sitting, no one is ever stiff, and it's virtually injury-free, without side effects. It's effective, too; people often feel better right away, giving them the confidence to keep doing good things for their body."

Healing, balancing and centering help the body, which is why Qi Gong is used in hospitals in China. At a Beijing rehabilitation hospital Rosanne visited, the research shows that cancer patients who practice Qi Gong need much less chemotherapy and have a higher rate of cure than other patients. "I received a lot of my training from the doctors there, as well as from the doctors in Beidehe, a research and rehabilitation hospital—one of only five approved Qi Gong training sites for doctors."

Qi Gong is a Chinese phrase for Taoist exercise that focuses on balancing and strengthening the flow of energy in one's body. It involves the total being, connecting body, mind, and spirit rather than targeting only one element, as is often the case in our culture. Also unlike Western culture, the Chinese believe illness is derived from a blocking of the Qi energy, which puts the body out of balance and makes one susceptible to a variety of health problems.

"I'm living proof Qi Gong exercises can be performed regardless of most prior health problems," Rosanne said. "There's certainly no guarantee that it will cure anything . . . but people feel better and heal faster, and that's a step in the right direction." Rosanne's students range in age from the mid-twenties to nineties. Some have been diagnosed with cancer and others have different problems. After suffering her own heart attack at 78, and the next year breaking a hip, Rosanne is living testament that Qi Gong has been an effective exercise for her.

"I've always been interested in staying healthy and know I can't do everything I used to, but I know I have to do something to keep my body moving. I've cut back my walking from five miles when I was in my seventies to just a couple of miles today. Combined with my yoga and Qi Gong, I feel just great, have no aches and pains and want others to feel this way too!"

Even with all her regular exercise, Rosanne knows she can't control everything that happens to her, but she can always work towards getting better. "I do take care of myself, take my medicine, eat healthy, and I feel alive and energetic, so I just go with the flow," she said. "Maybe one of the best things about getting older is we get more laid-back about things . . . it usually all works out O.K., so there's really no reason to worry."

Gordy Shields, 79

El Cajon, California

Thirty years ago, a diagnosis of bursitis and tendinitis changed his life. Three years ago, stenosis of the spine left him expecting to only be able to walk with a cane. Today, Gordy says he's in the best shape of his life!

He doesn't refer to any of this as a personal combat against age, but rather an example of the need for discipline in living an active, healthy life in spite of these existing health conditions. A lifelong passion for tennis was abruptly ended when Gordy's doctor told him it was ruining his shoulder. Suddenly, a vision of playing checkers and backgammon on the front porch entered his mind, yet that was definitely not part of his ideal retirement plan. "Once I accepted the fact that tennis was no longer going to be a part of my life, I knew I had to somehow find a new activity to fill that void," Gordy said. "I found cycling, and frankly don't know why I didn't discover it earlier, because it is something I'll be able to do for a lifetime and will continue to reap great physical benefits from as well."

Gordy has been the reigning national cycling champion for the 75-plus age group for the past four years and was only recently knocked out of the top spot. Perhaps one of the most amazing aspects of his success is his ability to perform competitively at this level, in spite of his existing spinal condition.

"Cycling is the reason I'm in such good shape—stenosis or not, bursitis, tendinitis, it doesn't matter, because none of it interrupts my ability to cycle—I can pedal with the best of them, generally averaging about

35 miles a day and around 120 to 150 miles per week . . . me and my two wheels, just pumping along."

Cycling is a growing sport among older adults and senior athletes across the country because it's gentle on the body—unless you crash, of course. Even with some of its danger and the riskiness of human flesh meeting pavement, the payoff and rewards of vitality, camaraderie, and good health far outweigh the risks, according to Gordy.

"You can't find a better environment or climate to be in for cycling than the mildness we enjoy here in San Diego. As a result, there are lots of older adults, particularly, who are avid cyclists here. In fact, our local Cyclo-Vets is the largest masters bicycling racing group in the United States, with more champions than any other group in the country."

It takes guts, too, which Gordy apparently has, because when he was 72, he suffered a life-threatening injury while riding. It is perhaps a cyclist's worst nightmare: the rider in front of him hit a pothole and Gordy was unable to maneuver away from the wreck. He hit the downed bike at 20 MPH and flew, head first, onto the pavement. His forehead hit the asphalt first, his helmet shattered and then he skidded on the right side of his face for about fifteen yards. He was in the hospital for two days, had a little plastic surgery and was back in the saddle again shortly thereafter.

"It was a fluke thing and I still believe the rewards of cycling far outweigh the risks—at least, this is my way of thinking," Gordy said. "I still love cycling and it makes me feel good, too, so I just keep on keeping on!"

Today, Gordy is a big advocate of cycling and enjoying life. He says when he goes to reunions his friends are always so amazed at how he has stayed in such good shape, and he tells them the same thing every time: "Pay attention to enjoying life and take care of yourself, because without your health there's not much left." He believes he inherited a good body and that it's his responsibility to take care of it. He says he tries to eat a good diet—doesn't make a fetish out of it, but does credit eating right to his wife, Olwyn, who he claims is a great cook.

"The recent studies regarding exercise and aging are just incredible, and it's very simple to age in good health by just paying attention to this stuff," Gordy said. "You need to find a level that is comfortable for you, stay with it, and just go for it, instead of being so sure you can't before you even try. 'I can't' just doesn't exist in my life—somehow, someway, I'll do it!"

As far as finding the secret of youth, Gordy says he never really left it behind. He says he forgets how old he is, has never felt old, and has no intention of experiencing it anytime soon. He will pedal until he can't anymore. Otherwise, those health problems may try to dictate his life, and he will have none of that—he's in control now, and that's the way he likes it.

Barbara Shirley, 81

San Diego, California

After she retired, Barbara went back to work. Not because she had to, but because she wanted to. Barbara is definitely a "people person," and although she's categorized as an "older worker," she's one of the store's top-producing employees even though she only works part-time.

"I was inspired to go back to work after retiring from twenty-years in the civil service," Barbara said. "My husband and I actually retired on the same day! We spent a few years playing golf and traveling, but when he decided to 'retire to the golf course,' I decided to retire to people!"

Few people look forward to a job interview, especially at the age of 68, but Barbara—admittedly a little unsure of what to expect—was just her typically positive self and was hired on the spot! Positive personalities do well in people-oriented positions, and age has little to do with these skills. In fact, age may actually work in Barbara's favor in this case—her life experience enables her to interact comfortably with people of all ages.

"I love the interaction with our customers. I'll see someone come in wearing a football jersey representing a certain team and just strike up a conversation with them—genuinely, because I love sports—and before you know it, we've got a rapport going. I don't ever look at people as a 'sale'; I just enjoy meeting them . . . and if I can help them find something they like, all the better."

The younger staff members can't believe her stamina. After spending all day on their feet, they are often the ones who complain of being tired. Meanwhile, Barbara's just movin' and groovin' her way all over the store. "It must be the shoes they wear . . . maybe they're uncomfortable. It's hard to be fashionable and comfortable, so I guess I've just found the right combination because I do my shift without too much difficulty."

Of course, Barbara takes care of herself and looks at least twenty years younger than her age, probably because of her diet and exercise. Suffering with polymyalgia rheumatica for more than a year, however, has forced Barbara to cut back on her walks from six days a week to two. It also requires medication, which she prided herself on never taking before. "I didn't take any pills before this condition, but I needed the medication to keep on living. It's getting better now, and the doctor is slowly weaning me off the prescription, so I'll be back to

100 percent again soon. But I've kept walking—even though I had to scale back. I insisted on doing it, and I know it's helped me heal and feel better, too."

Staying active, she says, is half the battle, because it helps keep her mind and body busy. Besides running all over the store, Barbara stays sharp mentally by working with numbers: prices, sales, discounts, and her customers' money. "Being involved in something gives you less time to worry about all the other things in your life. Sometimes it's easier to just sink down into the doldrums rather than pull yourself up and continue to march on."

Spoken like a true Navy wife and civil service retiree, Barbara speaks volumes by doing and being. She's fulfilled in life and attributes much of it to her loving husband of sixty years, Ben. She says she "hit the jackpot" when she married him. Together with three beautiful children and three grandchildren, they live a life of contentment and joy realizing they have every reason to be happy and positive.

"I think growing older is what we each make it. You can be happy or you can count the days until you die. I won't be doing any of that, though. I'm going to live out my days with all the life I can possibly fit in . . . and I plan to die with a smile on my face!"

Maja Sloss-Silberberg, 85

Valley Village, California

Her professional life revolved around prevention, so it is no surprise that she is continuing to share this important message with others. "I worked as a physical therapist for fifty years and believe me when I tell you it's essential to take care of your body all the way through your lifetime. It is even more important as we get older to prevent decline and gravity from taking over," Maja said.

She has been teaching her "Stay Fit" exercise class for more than twenty years. Fully aware of what can happen if one doesn't take care of the body, Maja knows that the decline so often accepted as a natural part of aging can be mitigated and so she has dedicated herself to help.

"Without proper posture, everyday movements like standing and sitting can create muscle strain, which will eventually lead to pain, then to people not doing anything. That's when the big trouble begins. I see so many older adults slumping over, almost like they're letting gravity pull them down, and then the body begins to cave in, too, followed by a host of physical and even psychological problems as a result."

Many take good health and strength for granted when they are younger and figure it's not possible to maintain or even attain a healthy, strong physique in their later years. However, it is now believed that you're never too old to feel better. The belief that decline is inevitable with age is outdated, and although Maja acknowledges that problems are more prevalent as one grows older, she also believes that if more people knew and understood what they could do to prevent these problems, there would be fewer people in pain.

"Feeling good has no age limit and proper exercise can help people experience it. But first you have to be honest enough with yourself to not use age as the excuse. As people begin to see the role they play in aging and incorporate these changes into their lives, they begin to feel the difference!"

She admits she is blessed with good health but makes no secret that she is proud of her age and will never let a number get in her way. She says people tell her she looks twenty years younger than she is, too.

"It's consistent with the way I feel," Maja said. "I don't feel old, but I know my limitations and don't overdo it. I love chocolate and ice cream too, but it's all about moderation. What does age have to do with that?"

John Smith, 84

Carlsbad, California

To find your soulmate in life is indeed a spiritual experience. When you lose them to death, it is that same spiritual connection that enables you to keep going in life . . . knowing that you will meet again, in a different place. John Smith speaks lovingly of his wife Ann, who he lost to cancer, after thirty years of marriage. He believes wholeheartedly that his spirituality and belief structure have contributed significantly to his healing after her death, making an even deeper impact on how he views his own mortality.

Having suffered a heart attack three years ago, John also knows his health is slowly failing—but he's still here and plans to live vibrantly every day. He credits much of this internal drive to his fearlessness about dying, due both to his spiritual way of life and his feeling of eternal connection with his soulmate Ann. The loss of a loved one and health changes are among the most difficult challenges people face. The feeling of losing control over one's life can be simply overwhelming and indeed one of the biggest fears that come with age. However John has chosen to live his life as an example to others on how to turn a negative into a positive.

"I could sit back and wallow in grief," John said . "But what good would that do—I'm still here and life is meant to be lived, so that's what I am doing." And living he is . . . he walks three miles a day, helps with his son's tennis program—batting around some four hundred tennis balls a day—goes to the beach, plays frisbee, keeps mentally active, and only takes medications to manage his heart condition.

"My heart attack was a wake-up call for me, and I realized I needed to get in better shape, physically, in order to have any life at all. There's no doubt in my mind, that this health regimen has contributed significantly to my current quality of life." He keeps himself mentally healthy through his lifelong passion for learning. A local community college hosts an Elderhostel class, LIFE (Learning, Inspiration, Fellowship and Enrichment), which provides the stimulation that has helped him adjust to the various changes in his life.

"This program has been great for me, and I would encourage anyone to get involved. It helps you focus and think about things other than your own problems. We discuss politics, scientific issues, health, books, computers, movies, volunteer opportunities, investments, travel destinations—just about anything you can think of!"

Additionally, John stays involved with one of his primary passions: flying. He retired at the age of 81 after thirty-six years as the superintendent of operations at Los Angeles International Airport. He also served as a flight instructor at Torrance and other local airports until he was 82. Now he enjoys flying with other qualified pilots, as well as practicing his own simulated flying and landings on his computer.

"It's not the same as flying, but it keeps me connected to something I really love," John said. "Flying was like a spiritual experience for me . . . I always felt closer to God when I was up in the wild blue yonder!"

John claims he feels great today and credits his strength to the balance he has found in his life. The physical, mental, emotional, and spiritual are all equal and necessary components to living a long, healthy, and active life so he encourages others to "tune in within" to establish the positive connection that life offers.

Gordon Spilker, 70

San Marcos, California

If you think kids are the only ones having fun these days, you'd better think again! The desire to have fun prompted Gordon to put on skates again . . . and now he's having a blast!

"I saw kids zipping around and it looked like fun, so I thought what the heck, I'm going to give it a whirl!" Gordon said, remembering his first encounter with in-line skates, or "blades". "Never lose the kidlike qualities of having fun—that's got nothing to do with age."

Don't confuse Gordon with the skaters competing in those new "X Games," because his style is a little more mellow. He does claim, though, that it's still great exercise, easy, and a heck of a lot of fun—so he regularly encourages other older adults to give it a try, too!

"I've been fairly successful at influencing others to try blading," said Gordon. "I think it's really helpful in improving balance, which can be a problem sometimes with age. The secret is learning how to fall correctly so you don't hurt yourself. You will fall—that's a given—you just need to learn how to do it less dangerously and wear the right protective equipment; then it's not a problem."

Gordon's initial thoughts about retirement centered on what in the world he was going to do with all that free time. Now he's involved in so many different things he has no idea how he ever had time for work! His favorite is teaching others how to rollerblade. "When I got started, there wasn't anyone to help me learn, so now I help others who are also just starting out," said Gordon.

Today he gives lessons at a local skate center near his home, and age isn't an issue because Gordon coaches people young and old—anyone interested in adding a little zip to their life. He's there to encourage, support, and motivate because he believes no one should let age get in the way of fun and good health.

"There's too much negative emphasis on aging. A lot of people who retire have the attitude of 'I've worked all my life and now it's time to rest—go hang out on the couch,' and I think that's wrong." Gordon is not immune to age-related health problems like high blood pressure, but his blading helps manage his condition. He also believes the other health benefits he gains make skating twice the fun!

"Our bodies were meant to move; the challenge is to find something you enjoy doing and to keep doing it," said Gordon. "It really doesn't matter what it is, but fun is always going to be a top priority for me!"

Just then, Gordon's attention was diverted toward a young man who wheeled in on a new gadget called the "California Chariot," a cross between a bike and a skateboard. As Gordon got a closer look, there was a gleam in his eye and he said, "Wow . . . now that looks like something new and fun I'd like to try!"

June Tatro, 85

Escondido, California

June can put her body in positions people half her age couldn't, and it's a practice she's performed for more than forty years. Today, she teaches other older adults about the health benefits of exercise and is a living testament that it definitely works.

When asked why she continues to teach exercise, her answer is very simple: "I see people improve and that motivates me. Plus, I've always loved to move my body, and the result has kept me healthy and feeling great so I want to share this with others!"

Part of her success in teaching older adults is being one herself. Often the image we have of exercising involves only young people. June believes this is changing. Certified with a lifetime credential in California as a specialized body-conditioning instructor, June has worked with literally hundreds of people, many who

have suffered for years with chronic arthritis pain and other problems and have accepted their conditions as part of the aging process.

"I tell them they don't have to accept it, that they can improve and lessen the pain and debilitation by exercising and getting their joints moving again," she said. "I've had people come in wheelchairs, and their doctors have told them they'll never walk again. Not only do they walk, they even dance! It's the endless sitting and not moving that can be the real problem, because you lose bone mass and muscle strength with inactivity. My goal is to try and turn that around!"

More and more studies show that exercise—the right type for one's condition—can reverse much of the physical decline often accepted as an inevitable with aging. People can improve by doing simple exercises in the chair or even the water, to get started, but the most important thing is to get started. "I never push people to come to class . . . they come because they feel better, and when they don't come, they feel the difference," June said. "Being able to move your body, having mobility, is especially critical because it can make the difference between being independent or not."

June emphasizes a total body workout in her classes—much of it often done from the chair. To prevent injuries, she starts with a gentle warm-up by getting blood into the muscles, and some stretching and flexibility work to keep the joints from getting stiff and to better manage arthritis. Then it's on to strength exercises to reverse the natural loss in muscle strength and bone density which puts people at risk for osteoporosis.

"This is one of the newest and most important elements in exercise physiology. Without muscle strength, bone mass, and flexibility, it makes it difficult to get in and out of bed, up from a chair, walk, climb stairs, carry packages, etc. And when one can no longer perform these activities of daily living, independence is lost, too."

The second half of June's class is low-impact aerobic exercises to work the heart muscle. This gets the blood pumping, and the more oxygen you take in, the better you feel. June's class concludes with deep breathing and relaxation through simple yoga movements.

"Exercise has a healing effect on the body and the mind," June said. "If you start feeling better physically, then you feel better mentally. And if you believe in your mind you can feel better, then you will do the exercises."

June enjoys ballroom dancing with her husband of sixty-two years, Harvey. Both have always been healthy and active, yet when Harvey required quadruple-bypass surgery about ten years ago, they realized just how precious life was and decided to make some changes. Cholesterol was the culprit in Harvey's situation—he was never overweight, but that didn't mean he wasn't at risk. Now they eat more fresh fruits and vegetables, whole grains from cereals and breads, and keep their fat intake down to around 10 percent of their daily calories. They believe in vitamins, and drink a lot of water, too, which most people don't get enough of.

"We have a strong family connection—two daughters and five grandchildren; we're active in our church and enjoy visiting with friends," June said. "But most important is having a positive attitude . . . an attitude of gratitude for what we have. Too many people feel like victims of the world, and that's just not a healthy way to live . . . it's the wrong way to think, because as Jesus said, 'As you believe it, it will be done for you,' so we try to keep positive thinking at the forefront of our minds, which reflects in our daily actions."

Milton Tepper, 83

Burbank, California

He's affectionately referred to as the "human tornado," an appropriate nickname describing the fury and pace with which he seeks to dispel the negative image of aging. His advocacy for seniors improves their quality of life, and the impact of his dedication to political and governmental issues surrounding seniors will continue long after he is gone.

Milton has personally survived the challenges that often come with age and is attuned to the reality many older adults face. At age 60, he was unexpectedly terminated from his job of twenty-one years and replaced by a younger worker.

"I've been there, I've seen it, I've heard it and I've lived through age discrimination," Milton said. "It was a real wake-up call, because once I experienced that, it opened up a whole new world which has fascinated and stimulated me ever since."

Although Milton lost his job at a time in life when he was at his peak professionally and at an age where it's often difficult to find work due to stereotypes of older workers, it was perhaps a blessing in disguise. Since then his contributions to legislation affecting senior citizens have been extraordinary.

Not certain how to begin his advocacy, he nonetheless pursued it in his typical voracious style. A research project at the University of Southern California's Andrus Gerontology Center intrigued him, so Milton checked it out and has been actively involved ever since, twenty-two years later. "I'd never even heard of the word gerontology—had no idea what it meant. But I know a lot about aging now, and there's a tremendous amount of work to be done." Today Milton is recognized across the country and in Washington, D.C., for his tenacity and advocacy work on behalf of seniors.

"It's absolutely essential to find something to do that is vital to others. Before I lost my job, I was somebody. Then suddenly I felt like nobody—it's a tremendous loss of self-esteem that can be very dangerous," he said. "Everyone wants to be needed. It should come as no surprise that one of the highest suicide rates in this country is that of white males over the age of 80. If people feel they're not needed, then why be around if nobody cares? That's why it's so important to do something of value, something you really enjoy, to give your life a continued sense of purpose—at least that is how it is for me."

Milton has lived up to his word. His list of contributions continues to grow. He has made a full-time job out of being a volunteer and serving as an extraordinary senior activist, with no time for work even if it was available. His involvement began with the volunteer program at Andrus. As a fixture there, Milton has served in a variety of capacities, ranging from chairman of the program, initiator, and board member of the Andus Volunteers Advocacy Committee to being a peer counselor at the Andrus Older Adult Center (where he co-wrote a manual on how to conduct senior counseling groups). Among his favorite work is interacting with students ranging from elementary to college levels in an effort to help them better understand aging and its possibilities.

"One of the funniest things I was ever asked by the kids was if wrinkles hurt—to which I quickly replied, 'only if I iron them!'" Milton laughed. "It's so important to interact with the schoolkids, because that may be the age where ageism really starts. Our volunteers go into the schools and talk with the students about what it means to grow older. And it's a good thing we're there, because most all of them think it's a time of decline, due mostly to the images from the media. Plus, few have grandparents around to learn from, so we try to provide that opportunity to experience a more diverse side of aging."

Although Milton's message in the classroom often brings lots of laughter, his work is definitely no laughing matter. He's made a difference in this world, and that is what matters. He serves on numerous advisory boards for multipurpose centers, home health services, adult care centers, interfaith councils, and elder abuse task forces. He's been involved with the Alzheimer's Association, County Commission on Aging, AARP Vote, and as a member of the Ombudsman Blue Ribbon committee. From healthcare reform, Medicare issues and Social Security, Milton's focus on aging issues has also played a significant part at the White House Conference on Aging.

Milton has not escaped the ravages of time—health has been a challenge in recent years. From Milton's perspective, however, that keeps life exciting—these are just new hurdles to overcome. Amazingly, he continues to jump them successfully. "Oh yeah, I've had cancer, been on chemotherapy—none of that will stop me though, it's just more of an inconvenience. It slows me down a bit, and I don't have time for that—there's too much to do," Milton said. "I just learn how to work around it."

Milton keeps on living because he keeps on contributing. He has helped hundreds of older Americans recognize the joy of living a long life, and he's led by example. "You can't think only about the past—that's what makes you old. I look forward to tomorrow and the future. There's nothing we can do about the past except learn from it. I wouldn't go back to my youth for all the tea in China! I accept the challenges of growing older and adjust. I just wish more people in this country would change their thinking about age. We are a diverse group of people with a variety of our experiences, and that's where wisdom comes in. I hope to see the day where people are judged on their value, abilities, and contributions—not their chronological age. Age is experience, and only from it, can true wisdom come."

Lowell Tozer, 76

San Diego, California

S ome speak of "the Midas touch," but when people talk about Lowell, they speak of "the special touch." His enthusiasm for cuddling babies is a true act of love, and it's one he says he would gladly pay to do if he didn't have the opportunity as a volunteer. Lowell is special, and he's found the perfect job: to cuddle and love premature babies as one of only three men enrolled in the University of California San Diego Medical Center's Cuddler's Program.

"I've always loved babies—ask my family," Lowell said. "We'll all be out together, at a restaurant or wherever, talking away, and all of a sudden I'll spot a baby across the room and they lose me. I become totally enthralled. My family just smiles and says, 'Oh, no . . .

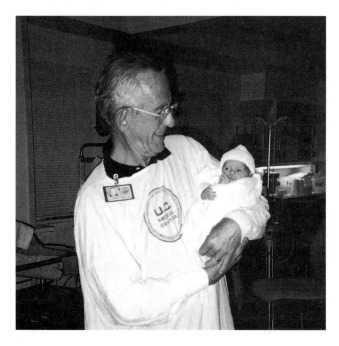

there goes Dad again . . . he's found another baby!'"

There's no question human touch is essential and even therapeutic for babies, but cuddling infants is not something you find many men doing. It seems more often this type of nurturing is done by women. "It isn't your typical macho occupation—but I believe there are many men like me out there who would love to be involved in something like this," Lowell said. "In fact, a newspaper article recently appeared about the male Cuddlers which swamped the hospital staff with phone calls from numerous other men who also wanted to get involved."

Call it luck, good timing, or maybe even divine intervention, because when Lowell called about the UCSD Cuddler program, not only was there a rare opening for a new volunteer, but the training course for the rookies was scheduled to begin the very next day. Lowell was definitely in the right place at the right time.

"This was my first volunteer job ever! And I'll tell you, if I had known I could be doing this in retirement, I would have retired a lot sooner! I started four years ago and they're going to have to kick me out, because I have no intention of ever leaving. In fact, the standard volunteer shift is three hours per week, but that just wasn't enough for me—I talked them into letting me come three days a week and I absolutely love it!"

Although Lowell recognizes that babies are his weakness, it is oftentimes the baby's weakness that really gets Lowell's attention. Whether it's those who are premature or those with serious medical problems, they all need loving and cuddling, and Lowell is always at the ready.

"We bundle them up in their blanket like a little burrito and hold them close to our bodies, which in my case radiates a lot of warmth because of my metabolism," Lowell explained. "And with the preemies [premature babies], sometimes I'll put a blanket over their head to block out the lights and whisper to them: 'we'll just pretend you're not born yet.'

Lowell also enjoys running and playing the piano. Although he's been on a two-year sabbatical from competitive running due to an annoying arthritic hip joint that the doctors say will only be repaired with replacement surgery, he is making a comeback with orthotics in his shoes and a couple of natural supplements that seem to be helping improve his condition.

Lowell keeps his brain busy, too, by playing the piano again after a forty-year lapse. He admits that he was fairly talented in his youth, and was amazed that his skills came back relatively easily, which proved to Lowell that mind and memory may not always decline over time. "I have a great memory . . . always did and still do! But I think staying engaged keeps you alive. Over the last three years I've been reading books on the mind and its abilities, which has led me to books on consciousness, evolution, quantum physics, and complexity theory. There's a definitely a connection between keeping your mind and body active throughout your lifetime, and continuing to learn, regardless of age. I can't imagine life without curiosity, keeping my brain and mind actively engaged."

Lowell admits that he has no idea what the secret to long life is, other than just taking care of yourself and staying involved. Giving is rewarding. "One of the most beneficial things in the world is giving love, so volunteering to love those babies is very fulfilling," Lowell said. "Sometimes I actually feel guilty because I think I'm getting more out of this than the babies. There seems to be a magical connection between us—I'm sure they sense I love them, because I really truly do!"

Warren Utes, 77

Park Forest, Illinois

I f you ever wondered whether there was a connection between exercise and mind power, just ask Warren Utes, who starts his day with a crossword puzzle and a run . . . and always in that order! "If I can't work out the puzzle, then I go workout my body! Then when I sit down again, I am usually able to complete the puzzle! Exercise circulates the blood and oxygen to all the cells, including those in the brain. As a result, the body and the mind get going, working properly and efficiently."

Efficient would be a good way to describe Warren, who has broken about every masters running record. "I started running at the age of 58, in the 1970s when the real running movement first began. Of course, there was speculation at that time about someone my age starting a physical sport like running, but I'm convinced it's why I'm still as healthy as I am today."

But Warren didn't start running competitively until he was 70, and since that time he has broken more than sixty-five records! Although he's become a legend in the running world due to his twelve national and world records for the men 75-plus age group, Warren doesn't consider himself extraordinary. As he looks ahead, he recognizes that the next age bracket starts at 80, so he has to stay in shape in order to start conquering that, and with his outlook and daily routine, it's likely he'll succeed.

"I'm pretty lazy other than my 6- or 9-mile run every day. You have to keep using your muscles, or they'll just waste away. I stretch too, because if I don't, I'm not sure if I'd be able to move the next day. I also concentrate on good nutrition, which my beloved wife of fifty years, Kay, has enabled me to do," Warren said. "We keep our daily fat intake low—stay away from animal fat, eat a lot of fruit, drink plenty of water and take a good multivitamin . . . no hidden magic or secret potions, just focus on the basics."

It's evident Warren leads his life by example, and in more ways than just at the starting line of a race. He's thankful for all he has and feels lucky to have been blessed with good health, even though he knows that running has contributed greatly to how he feels. He believes that his interest in competing and striving toward new goals, combined with the loving support from family and friends, have contributed to his amazing accomplishments and his aging process.

Jim Verdieck, 77

Poway, California

Do what you love, love what you do, and don't stop is the message from Jim. After fifty years of coaching tennis, one might think it's time to move on, but if you're happy and still contributing, isn't that what life is all about? Jim volunteers as the girls' tennis coach at the local high school, a position he has held for more than ten years. He's usually the first to arrive at the courts—even on his days off—and whichever girl gets to the courts first gets a special private lesson.

Coaching tennis has been Jim's life. He spent thirty-eight years at the University of Redlands, where his teams won more than nine hundred matches and fifteen NAIA and Division II National Championships. Facing retirement, Jim asked himself "Why stop doing something you enjoy just because you retire?"

His knees could be one answer, because they took the abuse of his hard-court life. He has had them both replaced, designed with matching vertical zippers down the front. They work great, too, so he can still be found hitting groundstrokes against the handball walls on campus.

His love for the game and continued involvement have really kept him going, and his drive and dedication have impressed the youngsters he's worked with as well. "He's my role model. When I get older, I'm not going to wither away and sit around doing nothing," said one of his students. "I'm staying involved!"

Jim feels fortunate to have a meaningful activity in his life that he can share with others. "If I can help someone else feel that same passion for tennis, then the satisfaction they get out of it is vicariously good for me too!"

Sister Monique Vredeveld, 70

Denver, Colorado

I t takes tremendous inner strength to watch your
family be tortured by Moslems and Japanese sol-
diers in concentration camps and to survive your
teenage years there, not knowing what tragedy the next
day would bring. Sister Monique is a survivor, and she
believes that those experiences helped to create the person she is today. Surviving Indonesia perhaps also prepared her for her next battle: shortly after arriving in the
United States she was diagnosed with cancer for which
she underwent eighteen surgeries; unbelievably, she was
declared cancer-free ten years later. Faith, she says, was
her most powerful strength, but inner peace and a
strong will to survive were also important tools that enabled her to overcome these extraordinary events.

"When I was first diagnosed with cancer, I worked
with a spiritual director who helped me realize that I
had buried my emotions and bad experiences from my
past and that I needed to release them from my mind
because they were possibly hurting my body," Sister
Monique said. "And as I started doing this, I felt a beautiful freedom that is hard to express, but it was like I
was releasing all these things I had been suppressing for
so long, and I do believe it aided my healing. I also had
a very strong desire to keep on living and this will to
live kept me alive."

Another significant factor in her recovery was her
love to run, which led her to being called "the Nun on
the run." "When I first came here, I remember seeing
lots of people in shorts and t-shirts running around. I
couldn't speak very good English, but I remember

asking them what it was they were doing, and before I knew it, I was out on the trail with them . . . running and absolutely loving it."

Sister Monique describes her daily running ritual as somewhat of a spiritual and meditative experience. It gives her time to tune in to her own body and think about the positive things, all the blessings in her life. "With all the negative cancer cells in my body, running was my positive balance. I really got hooked and truly believe to this day, that exercise was a big contributor to my healing—I just love it and it makes me feel joy in my heart."

Although after each cancer surgery she was only able to walk at first, within a relatively short period of time she'd be out running again, and it's a routine she's continued ever since. She logs a minimum of seven miles a day, rain or shine, sleet or snow. Her medicine is running.

She has become something of a celebrity on the running circuit by participating in weekend road races and winning numerous trophies and medals in her age group. She even runs half-marathons and still competes in about three of these thirteen-mile races every year.

"People always ask me how I do it and I just tell them the truth: I'm very relaxed and am only interested in enjoying myself and my life. Life is so short and I really want to enjoy it all the way through. I don't really see how you can enjoy life to the last minute by sitting on the couch — so I choose to be active."

And active she is. She doesn't have a car, so she bikes everywhere. Even if it takes her two to three hours to get places, she says she always feels great once she gets there. She just returned from a visit with her sister to Holland where they biked an average of 70 to 80 miles a day totaling four hundred miles in five days and staying overnight in youth hostels and farms along their way.

Regarding the aging process, she doesn't think much of it. "I never think of myself as 70 . . . never, never, never! People think they are old, but I tell them they're not and encourage them to sit around less and get up and get moving. Then they won't feel so old."

With all the extraordinary experiences she has faced, Sister Monique thinks that one of the most important things she's learned is not to feel sorry for yourself. "It seems that as people grow older, they start focusing on all the things that are wrong or negative in their lives,"

she said. "All that does is make them miserable and those around them miserable too. The next thing you know, you're in a pit and sometimes it's hard to get out."

Sister Monique has learned much from her life and believes she has received her strength and love from the Lord. She believes life is a gift—the most precious gift. "I live life the best I can and share the gift of life with others. I feel so happy. I must say, I really do enjoy life!"

Joe Weaver, 84

Dallas, Texas

At 65, Joe retired to "Cooper Town"—not the famous Baseball Hall of Fame in Cooperstown, New York, but the Cooper Fitness Center in Dallas, Texas. Established in 1970 by aerobics pioneer and best-selling author Kenneth H. Cooper, M.D., this multi-faceted organization is well known for its research in the areas of preventive health and innovative exercise programs, including the award-winning Cooper Classics Program for members age 55-plus.

"The Cooper Center is my home away from home," Joe said. "I signed up for all sorts of classes and activities, from bike, swim, and flexibility to walking and aquastrides. I go there three to four times a week, and combined with my daily yardwork, it's a good way to stay in shape."

Joe however, suffered with a common ailment that he also wanted to improve: low back pain. His doctor said the discs in his back were wearing out and he could expect to have pain. "I believed that there was some truth to that, but what I wouldn't accept that there wasn't anything I could do to improve it," Joe said. "I got a second opinion from a sports medicine orthopedist who, with a physical therapist, got me to a point where the pain was at least tolerable, and that was a definite improvement."

Since then, Joe has led a very active retirement lifestyle, but he can't help wonder what would have happened if he had not sought a second opinion from a physician who shared his philosophy. "Too many doctors today seem to believe that decline is inevitable with age and that nothing can be done about it."

Recently Joe developed a shoulder problem that required seeing the orthopedist again. Swimming and fishing seemed to aggravate it, so Joe knew he had to work on getting his flexibility back. "I talked to the people at Cooper about my condition, and they recommended I try the Tai Chi class. I remember my first day of class—we had an exercise where we were to raise our arms up over our head, and I couldn't possibly do it without excruciating pain. Yet when I realized I wasn't damaging anything further and that the pain was from the lack of flexibility and range of motion in that shoulder, I just slowly kept at it, stretching it every which way, and within a couple of months my shoulder was back to 95 percent!"

Tai Chi has become an increasingly popular form of exercise and rehabilitation for older adults. It focuses primarily on stretching, strengthening, and flexibility movements for muscles and joints. Its very foundation emphasizes the importance of relaxation and breathing exercises, which provide a good mental state for full concentration on the healing task at hand. Although this form of exercise has been practiced for years in Eastern cultures, it is a relatively new concept here in the West which is quickly growing in popularity as people learn more about its benefits.

"Probably most people are like me. I didn't know enough about Tai Chi and thought of it strictly as a relaxing stretch class. That couldn't be further from the truth—it's a real workout, as I am often sweating profusely by the end of each session."

Joe has learned that there are a variety of activities which can really make a difference in people's lives, and although the activities won't necessarily cure a health condition, they can help lessen the discomfort and even provide an opportunity to work toward improving it so that the pain and lack of mobility won't take over and create more health problems. "Too often people suffer with a health condition they feel they have no control over," Joe said. "Like my wonderful wife Mary Lou, 84, who I have been married to for sixty-three years. She has suffered with severe rheumatoid arthritis since the young age of 28. She knew she had to keep moving to prevent the condition from getting worse, and with her doctors she devised a plan that has enabled her to do so. The doctors told her that she would have been dead or in a wheelchair years ago if it were not for exercise."

It's all about finding the right type of exercise or activity for each person's specific conditions. Perhaps the type of activity will be something entirely different from what you've done before, but the reality is that you have to do something physical each and every day: move it or lose it.

Lucy White, 77

Jacksonville, Florida

Fun is the operative word in Lucy's life, and she honestly admits that her later-in-life passion has been the ride of her life. Lucy is something of a thrill-seeker enthusiast! Since starting her roller coast riding hobby in her sixties, she's ridden at least two hundred different roller coasters all over the world. Enthusiasts don't just ride it once, either. They usually make a day of it, logging in about ten rides per roller coaster, which means Lucy's taken some two thousand rides—and mostly from the front seat, too!

Although she claims her age is "39 and holding," how many people do you know, regardless of age, who could stomach this type of activity? Perhaps this new-found adventure is part of her secret to making her feel younger! "I never think about my age; I just like doing

things that are new and different—roller coasters and thrill rides definitely fall into that category!" Lucy laughed.

She remembers how she first got hooked, and it's not the typical way you might expect. In 1979, while watching a television special on roller coasters, the camera was attached to the front of "The Beast" at Kings Island, in Ohio. Lucy experienced the whole ride from her living room, watching it on TV. "That was the greatest thing ever, and I knew right then and there that I wanted to ride it and any others everywhere, too. Eventually I found out about the American Coaster Enthusiasts group, joined on the spot, and the fun began."

Her first adventure with the club was one she'll never forget: they went to Canada to ride "The Comet" at Crystal Beach, and Lucy believes it's undoubtedly one of the best coasters ever. "The dips and turns and negative-Gs [which coaster enthusiasts refer to as the sensation of being lifted out of your seat] were just incredible!" Lucy said with an excitement level that would make you think it was something she did just yesterday instead of thirteen years ago. "Of course, 'The Cyclone' at Coney Island in New York is also right up there in the rankings of the 'incredibleness' factor!"

Just last year she traveled with the club in England, with four bus loads of members from all over the country. "We did twelve parks in ten days, including our rides on the 'Mega-Phobia' coaster in Wales, which is one of those good old-fashioned wooden ones. It's really like a different ride each time due to its wood structure, which gives and changes a bit with the weather and each time around."

Although Lucy is one of the oldest members of the club, she doesn't see what age has to do with having fun. She figures that one of the reasons she's doing this is she didn't get the chance to do it when she was younger. Her parents never allowed her to ride roller coasters as a child, and she thinks it was because they were afraid to go on the ride.

"When my grandchildren were younger, we would go together all the time. In fact, when my granddaughter was in the third grade she wrote an essay about our fun and titled it 'Roller Coaster Grandma!' It was so good, *Roller Coaster Magazine* published it in one of their issues," Lucy said.

As for her philosophy on aging, she firmly believes that this love of coaster riding has been a positive in helping her overcome the negatives that so often surround the concept of growing older. "There's a saying I sort of live by: 'I don't mind growing older, I just don't want to get old!,' and I think that's a pretty good motto! This gives me something to look forward to; it's an interest I share with others, something I plan for, and indeed something that excites me. I do what I love and love what I do! People often ask me why I do it, and I tell them because it's there. It's true: I really can't go anywhere that has a roller coaster and not get on it!"

With the increasing number of roller coasters and thrill rides across the country, it's evident that Lucy has chosen a hobby that will last a lifetime. "Each ride is like a shot of adrenaline to me!" Lucy laughed. So next time you board a thrill ride or roller coaster, don't be surprised if you see Lucy sitting up there in the front row waiting for the fun to begin!

Spiegle Willcox, 94

Cincinnatus, New York

The tone from his trombone is as smooth to the ear as silk is to the touch. To say he's still got it doesn't even do him justice; to say he's a legend is obvious. With 83 years of experience, Spiegle is definitely among the best of the best. In his earlier days, he replaced Tommy Dorsey in the famed Victor Recording band of Jean Goldkette to sit alongside Bix Beiderbecke and Frank Trumbauer. He earned Goldkette's accolade as "the best trombonist I ever had," a tribute Spiegle cherishes and has in writing.

Spiegle's still at it today—he performs at various jazz festivals in Europe and America, where he's been asked

to tour and share his special gift. Much like a fine wine, Spiegle seems to get better with time. "There's something about music that moves the soul—it's ageless," said Spiegle. "Music has definitely been good to me; so if I can continue to share its magic with others, then that makes life worth living."

His fans come in droves to all of his gigs. Young and old alike, Spiegle continues to delight them with more than just music—he sings and tells stories, too! Although jazz instrumentalists are not usually known for their singing, Spiegle's still got it, and you'd never guess he's in his nineties.

"Playing the trombone is a good workout," Spiegle said. "It's not the easiest instrument to play, but I've still got my lungs and wind ability to blow it out there— even my upper body gets a workout with all that sliding! But most importantly, I still enjoy it, and that's what really matters. You've got to keep doing the things you love as long as you can. Staying involved with a passion has played a big part in my longevity."

Spiegle continues to balance his love of music with his love of family and friends, maintaining strong ties with the local clan. In fact, all his relatives live within a thirty-mile radius, and although he lost his spouse twelve years ago, he cherishes her memory and the sixty wonderful years they had together.

"One reason I'm still alive today is because I don't think much about when it will end. It's not that I'm afraid to die, it's just that I don't want to be there when it happens," Spiegel laughed. "But of course, as I've always said . . . old trombone players never die . . . they just slide away."

Jean Wright-Elson, 69

San Diego, California

She believes the word "retire" should be changed to "regroup," since it's more reflective of what takes place during this phase of life. Retirement is by no means an end, but rather a time for new beginnings—a time to do the things you've always wanted to do. "I look at retirement as an opportunity to further my own personal growth . . . spiritually, mentally, and physically," Jean said.

From marking each birthday and its passage of time by embarking on new and different challenging adventures, to establishing programs that improve the lives of others and benefit the community, Jean is something of a risk-taker and immensely enjoys the thrill that comes with it. "I guess it's part of my innate personality, to test myself and see what's possible. I think we grow when we challenge ourselves."

Jean knows all about challenges and believes they should be viewed as positive opportunities. She spent her professional career serving in the Air Force Nurse Corps and continued her contributions to the health field in retirement. She developed the first prenatal nurse clinic in the state of Texas at the Robert B. Green Hospital in San Antonio and served ten years as a volunteer with the San Diego Hospice, where she developed the first "laugh library" for patients and staff. Most recently Jean established the first parish nurse program for her four- thousand-member church.

"This became a vision of mine, a calling to develop this for our congregation because I feel strongly about the importance of our members' health," Jean said. "In addition to conducting regular health screenings, we provide seminars on preventive health issues. People need to realize that about 75 percent of the illnesses we have are related to our lifestyle choices and decisions we make about proper diet, exercise, smoking, and drinking. We all have a physician within us that we need to pay attention to, because our body can regulate itself if given the chance. It's not the doctor's job alone to take care of us; we play an important role too."

Jean uses the analogy of the body as a temple. "Most people wouldn't trash a temple or sanctuary of worship—so is it O.K. to trash our bodies with improper lifestyle choices? That just doesn't make sense—both are gifts of God and should be treated with great respect."

Jean thinks humor is really important, too, and it may even be a little misunderstood as far as its therapeutic value. "Studies have continually shown that humor can diminish a person's pain and increase endorphins, which generally make one feel better. Humor is all around us, and sometimes we are our own best material!"

Jean leads by example, and it's often her travel adventures that conjure up the biggest smiles. She believes life is a journey, and not a guided tour so Jean's certainly not the cruise-ship type. She likes a little excitement that generally carries the slightest bit of risk or challenge with it, to make it really fun. "I just returned from Borneo—a hiking trek through the rainforest. I figure if I'm going to be the parish nurse who advocates exercise, I have to be a good role model too! Last year I lived on a barge and bicycled along the dikes and through the tulip fields in Holland. The year before I biked along the Danube from Passau, Germany to Vienna, Austria. I also spent a week petting whales at the San Ignacio La goon—so I like to do different things, and all are definitely new growth experiences, too!"

She's parasailed in San Diego, shot the rapids in the Grand Canyon, kayaked in Baja California, scuba dived in Tahiti, soloed a glider plane over Warner Springs, and even experienced an African photo safari in Kenya—all after the age of 55. "Age is a celebration of life. Each birthday represents a new year for adventure and growth. For my 70th, I plan to scuba dive on the Great Barrier Reef in Australia!"

Birthdays also represent a time to reflect on the true meaning of life . . . to plan the days ahead, to regroup, and to reach for new goals. With a strong spiritual foundation as her continual guide, Jean's life will always be the real adventure.

"Toodie" Audrey Wright, 71

Spring Valley, California

I t was her 70th birthday, and banners and balloons filled the room. Over in the corner was something big, shiny, and new—just what she'd wished for: a basketball hoop and backboard too! "It was the thrill of my life and I shrieked with delight, like when a kid gets a new bike!" Toodie said. "It was a gift from my three daughters and my grandchildren, too—it gets put to good use, I can certainly tell you!" She picked up the game of hoops later in life, although it was always something that intrigued her. "Growing up in the midwest, girls were never encouraged to play basketball in those days, competitively or any other way, for that matter."

But women's sports were her destiny, because Toodie's three daughters were athletically inclined and she found herself involved with their sports, including managing a number of softball teams—which just may have been the beginning of what lay ahead.

"Once my children were grown and gone, I needed something to do on my own. My husband had died, so I was really on my own, and although active with my work, church, and friends, I was still searching for something . . . I just didn't know what."

Ideas seem to come from the strangest places, and while Toodie was attending a baby shower she heard about a new Senior Women's Basketball League. Before long, Toodie was getting directions for the next practice. "The league was only a couple of years old at the time so they were looking for new players, especially women over 65. Thank goodness I was old enough to play; imagine that—an activity that rewards you for being older!" she laughed. "Of course I loved it—the ladies were super; we had a great time, and I was immediately welcomed and embraced by new friends!"

The first year on the team was a great deal of fun. There were regular practices and workouts to attend, but there was also a special bond and camaraderie these women shared. Whatever it was it must have been right, because Toodie and her new teammates played in the Senior Olympics that very same year.

"Our league sent six teams to Tucson for the U.S. National Senior Sports Classic, and my team came home with a silver medal in the 65-plus age division. We lost the gold by only one point in the championship game. We so wanted that little gold medal, not just for us, but for our coach too," Toodie said.

In a basketball league with players' ages ranging from 50 to 70-plus and all of them women, this would not be the place you would expect to find a male

"Toodie" Audrey Wright, second from left

teenager, but the coach behind this silver-medaling championship team was just seventeen. And Justin, it seems, learned an early life lesson: there's definitely more to sports than merely one's age. "Age is obviously not only measured in years, because none of these women say they feel like their age," Justin said on the *NBC Nightly News* telecast with Tom Brokaw. "They're competitive and want to win just like people at any age."

It's more than competition and camaraderie that make these women go—there are health benefits, too. "Even though there are sore days, I really feel great" Toodie said. "My energy is better, and I know that getting out and moving my body on a regular basis is benefiting me physically. If I didn't have this, I might see little reason to get out of my pj's every morning. I don't want to sit home and watch TV, nor do I want to bug my kids. They've got their lives to live and we want to live ours."

Their families and friends are very supportive and proud and can often be found in the motorhome caravan when teams travel to various competitions. Some think they're nuts—while others are simply amazed. "I know people are definitely surprised because I hear from them all when we're on TV! I don't talk much about it, but maybe I should, because like me, I bet more people would play if they knew that they could! None of us ever dreamed we'd be doing this now, but just look at us—we're simply having a ball!"

Toodie recognizes the importance of being engaged in an activity or hobby that brings joy and meaning to her life. She still works part-time with special-education students where she taught school for twenty-three years, and she believes that being around people, helping and contributing, keeps her spirit alive.

"It's like magic! It kind of makes your troubles disappear. We all have a variety of problems we could think about all day. I don't know anyone who doesn't have some type of health hassle, whether it's asthma like me, or diabetes and arthritis. We know we can't make all our problems go away forever, but for some reason when I'm out on the court or volunteering, my troubles do go away . . . even if it is only for a short while."

So birthdays will continue to be a celebration of life, a time full of magic and wishes to come true, and for that very reason, Toodie looks forward to the next time she hears, "Happy Birthday to You!"

Bortz, Walter M., II. *Dare to Be 100*. New York: Simon & Schuster Inc., 1996.

———. *We Live Too Short and Die Too Long*. New York: Bantam Books, 1991.

Clark, Etta. *Growing Old Is Not for Sissies II*. Rohnert Park, Calif.: Pomegranate Artbooks, 1995.

Cooper, Ken. *Advanced Nutritional Therapies*. Nashville, Tenn.: Thomas Nelson Publisher, 1996.

———. *Can Stress Heal?* Nashville. Tenn.: Thomas Nelson Publisher, 1997.

Dychtwald, Ken, and Joe Flower. *Age Wave*. Los Angeles: Jeremy P. Tarcher, Inc., 1989.

Evans, William, and Irwin H. Rosenberg. *Biomarkers*. New York: Simon & Schuster Inc., 1991.

Friedan, Betty. *The Fountain of Age*. New York: Simon & Schuster Inc., 1993.

Goldman, Connie, and Richard Mahler. *Secrets of Becoming a Late Bloomer*. Walpole, N. H.: Stillpoint Publishing, 1995.

Hayflick, Leonard. *How and Why We Age*. New York: Ballantine, 1994.

Nelson, Miriam E. *Strong Women Stay Young*. New York: Bantam Books, 1997.

Ornish, Dean. *Love and Survival*. New York: HarperCollins, 1998.

Rowe, John W. *Successful Aging*. New York: Pantheon Books, 1998.

Schachter-Shalomi, Zalman, and Ronald S. Miller. *From Age-ing To Sage-ing*. New York: Warner Books, 1995.

Sheehy, Gail. *New Passages*. New York: Random House, 1995.

Weil, Andrew. *Spontaneous Healing*. New York: Alfred A. Knopf, Inc., 1995.

(AARP) American Association of Retired Persons
601 E Street NW, Washington, D.C. 20049
800-424-3410 • 202-434-2277

Adventure Cycling Association
P.O. Box 8308-P, Missoula, MT 59807
406-721-1776

Aerobics and Fitness Association of America
15250 Ventura Boulevard, Ste. 200, Sherman Oaks, CA 91403
818-905-0040

Amateur Athletic Union (AAU)
Walt Disney Resorts
P.O. Box 10000, Lake Buena, Vista FL 32830
407-363-6170

Amateur Speedskating Union of the United States
1033 Shady Lane, Glen Ellyn, IL 60137-4822
630-790-3230

American Academy of Medical Acupuncture
Referral to local affiliate
800-521-2262

American Alliance for Health, Physical Education,
Recreation and Dance
1900 Association Drive, Reston, VA 20191
703-476-3400

American Alpine Club
710 10th Street, Golden CO 80401
303-384-0110

American Association of Cardiovascular and
Pulmonary Rehabilitation
7611 Elmwood Avenue, Ste. 201, Middleton, WI 53562
608-831-6989

American Bowling Congress
5301 S. 76th Street, Greendale, WI 53129
414-421-6400

American Cancer Society
  1599 Clifton Road NE, Atlanta, GA 30329-4251
  800-227-2345 • 404-320-3333

American College of Sports Medicine
  P.O. Box 1440, Indianapolis, IN 46206-1440
  800-486-5643 • 317-637-9200

American College of Surgeons
  55 E. Erie Street, Chicago, IL 60611
  312-202-5000

American Council on Exercise (ACE)
  5820 Oberlin Drive, Ste. 102, San Diego, CA 92121
  800-825-3636 • 619-535-8227

American Diabetes Association
  1660 Duke Street, Alexandria, VA 22314
  800-DIA-BETES

American Dietetic Association
  216 W. Jackson Boulevard, Ste. 800, Chicago, IL 60606-6995
  800-366-1655

American Foundation for the Blind
  15 W. 16th Street, New York, NY 10011
  800-232-5463

American Geriatrics Society
  770 Lexington Avenue, Ste. 300, New York, NY 10021
  212-308-1414

American Heart Association
  Referral to local affiliate
  800-242-8721 • 214-706-1936

American Lung Association
  1740 Broadway, New York, NY 10010
  212-315-8700

American Medical Association (AMA)
515 N. State Street, Chicago, IL 60610
800-621-8335

American Occupational Therapy Association, Inc.
P.O. Box 31220, Bethesda, MD 20824-3122
301-652-2682

American Orthopaedic Society for Sports Medicine (AOSSM)
6300 N. River Road, Ste. 200, Rosemont, IL 60018
847-292-4900

American Parkinson's Disease Association
60 Bay Street, Ste. 401, Staten Island, NY 10301
800-223-2732

American Physical Therapy Association
1111 N. Fairfax Street, Alexandria, VA 22314
703-684-2782

American Platform Tennis Association
P.O. Box 43336, Upper Montclair, NJ 07043
973-744-1190

American Racewalk Association
P.O. Box 4, Paonia, CO 81428
970-527-4557

American Running and Fitness Association
4405 East-West Highway, Ste. 405, Bethesda, MD 20814-1621
301-913-9517

American Self-Protection Association, Inc. (Judo, Aikido, Tai Chi)
825 Greengate Oval, Sagamore Hills, OH 44067
330-467-1750

American Society on Aging
833 Market Street, Ste. 500, San Francisco, CA 94103
415-974-9600

American Society of Biomechanics
   128 Guggenheim, Mayo Clinic, Rochester, MN 55905
   507-284-2262

American Swim Coaches Association
   301 SE 20th Street, Ft. Lauderdale, FL 33316
   954-462-6267

American Water-Ski Association
   799 Overlook Drive, Winterhaven, FL 33884
   800-533-2972

Arthritis Foundation
   1314 Spring Street, Atlanta GA 30309
   800-283-7800

Be Fit Enterprises—Jack LaLanne Products
   P.O. Box 1023, San Luis Obispo, CA 93406
   805-772-6000

California Parks and Recreation Society
   916-665-2777 • www.cprs.org

California State University Fullerton (CSUF)
   Lifespan Wellness Center, Fullerton CA 92634
   714-278-2620

Centers for Disease Control and Prevention
   1600 Clifton Road NE, Atlanta, GA 30383
   888-232-4674 • 404-639-3311

Center for the Study of Aging
   706 Madison Avenue, Albany, NY 12208
   518-465-6927

Cooper Institute for Aerobic Research
   12330 Preston Road, Dallas, TX 75230
   972-341-3200

Disabled Sports USA
   451 Hungerford Drive, Ste. 100, Rockville, MD 20850
   301-217-0960

Elderhostel
75 Federal Street, Boston, MA 02110-1941
617-426-8056 • 617-426-7788

Fifty-Plus Fitness Association
Box D, Stanford, CA 94309
650-323-6160 • www.50plus.org

Foster Grandparent Program
Referral to local affiliate
800-424-8867

Gerontologic Society of America
1275 K Street NW, Ste. 350, Washington, D.C. 20005
202-842-1275

Governor's Council on Physical Fitness and Sports
201 S. Capitol Avenue, Ste. 560, Indianapolis, IN 46225

Grandparents United for Children's Rights, Inc.
137 Larkin Street, Madison, WI 53705
www.sedun@inexpress.net

Grandtravel (Intergenerational Vacations)
6900 Wisconsin Avenue, Ste. 706, Chevy Chase, MD 20815
800-247-7651

Gray Panthers
2025 Pennsylvania Ave NW, Ste. 821, Washington, D.C. 20006
800-280-5362

Ice Skating Institute
355 W. Dundee Road, Buffalo Grove, IL 60089
847-808-7528

International Association of Fitness Professionals
6190 Cornerstone Court East, Ste. 204, San Diego, CA 92121
619-535-8979

(IHRSA) International Health, Racquet and Sportsclub
   Association
   263 Summer Street, Boston, MA 02210
   800-228-4772

International Jugglers Association
   P.O. Box 218, Montague, MA 01351
   413-367-2401

International Physical Fitness Association
   415 W. Court Street, Flint, MI 48503
   810-239-2166

International Swimming Hall of Fame
   One Hall of Fame Drive, Ft. Lauderdale, FL 33316
   954-462-6536

International Weightlifting Association
   P.O. Box 444, Hudson, OH 44236
   330-655-9644

Jazzercise, Inc.
   2808 Roosevelt Street, Carlsbad, CA 92008
   760-434-2101

Men's Senior Baseball League
   1 Huntington Quadrangle, Ste. 3N07, Melville, NY 11747
   516-753-6725

National Alliance for Senior Citizens
   1700 18th Street NW, Washington, D.C. 20009
   202-986-0117

National Association of Area Agencies on Aging
   1112 16th Street NW, Ste. 100, Washington, D.C. 20036-4823
   202-296-8130

National Association of Senior Friends
   P.O. Box 1300, Nashville, TN 37202
   800-348-4886

National Association of State Units on Aging
    12251 I Street NW, Ste. 725, Washington, D.C. 20005-3914
    202-898-2578

National Congress of State Games and Member States
    401 Ninth 31st Street, Billings, MT 59101
    406-254-7426

National Council on Aging
    409 Third Street SW, Washington, D.C. 20024-3212
    202-289-6976

National Council on Senior Citizens
    1331 F Street NW, Washington, D.C. 20004
    202-347-8800

National Eye Institute—Information Office
    31 Center Drive, MSC 2510, Bethesda, MD 20892-2510
    301-496-5248

National Head Start Association
    1651 Prince Street, Alexandria, VA 22314
    703-739-0875

National Horseshoe Pitchers Association
    3085 76th Street, Franksville, WI 53126
    414-835-9108

National Institute on Aging
    Box 8057, Gaithersburg, MD 20858
    800-222-2225 • 301-496-1752

National Masters News
    (Track and Field, Long-Distance, Racewalking)
    P.O. Box 50098, Eugene OR 97405
    541-343-7716

National Osteoporosis Foundation
    1150 17th Street NW, Ste. 500, Washington, D.C. 20036-4603
    202-223-2226

National Recreation and Park Association
2775 S. Quincy Street, Ste. 300, Arlington, VA 22206
703-858-0784

National Senior Games Headquarters
Referral to local affiliate
800-331-9211

National Senior Pro Rodeo Association
P.O. Box 316, Roundup MT 59072
406-323-3380

National Senior Service Corps Hotline
Referral to local affiliate
800-424-8867

National Senior Sports Association
83 Princeton Avenue, Hopewell, NJ 08525
800-282-6772

National Society to Prevent Blindness
500 E. Remington Road, Schaumberg, IL 60173
800-331-2020

National Strength and Conditioning Association
P.O. Box 38909, Colorado Springs, CO 80937
719-632-6722

National Stroke Association
300 E. Hampton Avenue, Englewood, CO 80110
303-649-9060

North American Senior Circuit Softball
1204 W. 46th Street, Richmond, VA 23225
804-231-4254

North American Telemark Organization
Box 44, Waitsfield, VT 05673
800-835-3404

(OASIS) Older Adult Services and Information Services
7710 Carondelet, Ste. 125, St. Louis, MO 63105
314-862-2933

Older American's Volunteer Programs Office
1100 Vermont Avenue NW, 6th Fl., Washington, D.C. 20525
202-606-1855

Older Women's League (OWL)
666 11th Street NW, Ste. 700, Washington, D.C. 20001
800-825-3695

Professional Bowlers Association of America
1720 Merriman Road, Akron, OH 44334
330-836-5568

Project P.A.C.E
(Physician-Based Assessment and Consultant for Exercise)
San Diego State University, Department of Psychology
619-594-5949

Rails to Trails Conservancy
(Converts abandoned rail corridors to trails)
1400 16th Street NW, Ste. 300, Washington, D.C. 20036
202-331-9696

Road Runners Club of America
1150 S. Washington Street, Ste. 250, Alexandria, VA 22314
703-836-0558

(RSVP) Retired and Senior Volunteer Program
Corporation for National Service
1201 New York Avenue, NW, Washington, D.C. 20525
800-424-8867

Senior Athletes Hall of Fame
723 Oakview Drive, Bradenton, FL 34210
941-756-8808

Senior Olympics
Senior Games Association, National Headquarters
445 North Boulevard, Ste. 2001, Baton Rouge, LA 70802
504-379-7337

Senior Net
399 Arguello, San Francisco, CA 94188
415-352-1210

Senior Softball USA Inc.
9 Fleet Court, Sacramento, CA 95831
916-393-8566

Service Corps of Retired Executives/Small Business
Administration
409 Third Street SW, Washington, D.C. 20024
202-205-6762

Special Olympics International
1325 G Street NW, Ste. 500, Washington, D.C. 20005
202-628-3630

Sporting Goods Manufacturers Association
200 Castlewood Drive, North Palm Beach, FL 33408
561-842-4100

Triathlon Federation USA
3595 E. Fountain Boulevard, F-1, Colorado Springs, CO 80910
719-597-9090

United Parkinson's Foundation
833 W. Washington Blvd., Chicago, IL 60607
312-733-1893

U.S.A. Hockey, Inc.
4965 N. 30th Street, Colorado Springs, CO 80919
719-576-8724

U.S.A. Karate Federation, Inc.
1300 Kenmore Boulevard, Akron, OH 44314
330-753-3114

U.S.A. Softball
2801 NE 50th Street, Oklahoma City, OK 73111
405-424-5266

U.S.A. Volleyball
3595 E. Fountain Boulevard, Ste. I–2, Colorado Springs,
CO 80910
719-637-8300

United Square Dancers of America, Inc.
8913 Seaton Drive, Huntsville, AL 35802
205-881-6044

U.S. Administration on Aging
330 Independence Avenue SW, Washington, D.C. 20547-0008
202-619-0724

U.S. Aikido Federation
98 State Street, Northhampton, MA 01060
413-586-7122

U.S. Amateur Ballroom Dancers Association
P.O. Box 428, New Freedom, PA 17439
800-447-9047

U.S. Amateur Confederation of Roller Skaters
(Roller and In-Line Skating)
P.O. Box 6579, Lincoln, NE 68506
402-483-7551

U.S. Badminton Association
One Olympic Plaza, Colorado Springs, CO 80909
719-578-4808

U.S. Cerebral Palsy Athletic Association
200 Harrison Street, Newport, RI 02840
401-848-2460

U.S. Croquet Association
11585-B Polo Club Road, Wellington, FL 33414
561-753-9141

U.S. Field Hockey Association
   One Olympic Plaza, Colorado Springs, CO 80909
   719-578-4567

(USFSA) U.S. Figure Skating Association
   20 First Street, Colorado Springs, CO 80906
   719-635-5200

U.S. Golf Association (USGA)
   P.O. Box 708, Far Hills, NJ 07931
   908-234-2300

U.S. Judo Association
   21 North Union Blvd., Colorado Springs, CO 80919
   719-633-7750

U.S. Masters Swimming
   2 Peter Avenue, Rutland, MA 01543
   508-886-6631

U.S. National Senior Sports Organization
   1307 Washington Avenue, Ste. 706, St. Louis, MO 63103
   504-379-7337

U.S. Olympic Committee Sports Medicine Society
   1 Olympic Plaza, Colorado Springs, CO 80909-5760
   719-578-4546

U.S. Professional Tennis Association (USPTA)
   3535 Briarpark Drive, Houston, TX 77402
   713-978-7782

U.S. Rowing Association
   201 S. Capitol Avenue, Ste. 400, Indianapolis, IN 46225
   317-237-5656

U.S. Slo-Pitch Softball Association
   3935 S. Crater Road, Petersburg, VA 23805
   804-732-4099

U.S. Squash Racquets Association
23 Cynwyd Road, P.O. Box 1216, Bala Cynwyd, PA 19004
610-667-4006

U.S. Synchronized Swimming
201 S. Capitol Avenue, Ste. 510, Indianapolis, IN 46225
317-237-5700

U.S. Tennis Association (USTA)
70 W. Red Oak Lane, White Plains, NY 10604
914-696-7000

U.S. Walking Federation
4831 NE 44th Street, Seattle, WA 98105
206-524-6081

University of Southern California (USC)
Leonard Davis School of Gerontology
Andrus Volunteer Center
University Park, MC 0191, Los Angeles, CA 90089-0191
213-740-6060

Wheelchair Sports, USA
3595 E. Fountain Boulevard, Ste. L–1, Colorado Springs,
CO 80910
719-574-1150

Women's Sports Foundation
Eisenhower Park, East Meadow, NY 11554
516-542-4700

World Football Association
P.O. Box 775208, Steamboat Springs, CO 80477
303-278-9797

World Masters Cross-Country Ski Association
P.O. Box 5, Bend, OR 97709
541-382-3505

YMCA of the USA
101 N. Wacker Drive, Chicago, IL 60606
800-872-9622 • 312-977-0031

Attoun, Marti. "The Granny Who Made the Grade." *Good Housekeeping* (June 1997).

Banner, Margo. "Surfing Senior Makes Waves for 60 Years." *Blade-Citizen,* June 6, 1990.

Barry, John. "Aging Is Being Redefined." *San Diego Union-Tribune,* March 15, 1998.

Basheda, Lori. "Above It All." *Orange County Register,* July 23, 1997.

Berliner, Uri. "Strike Zone." *San Diego Union-Tribune,* February 27, 1995.

Bieze, Jordana. "Fit Escondido Resident Bending Perceptions of Old-age Limitations." *San Diego Tribune,* July 12, 1990.

Bluethman, Angie. "Out of this World." *San Diego Union-Tribune,* April 30, 1997.

Bond, Ed. "Age, Tragedy Can't Stop Fitness Trainer". *Los Angeles Times,* November 14, 1996.

Brooks, Jeanne Freeman. "Big Step Taken Back toward Normandy." *San Diego Union Tribune,* February 20, 1994.

———. "The Years Disappear as She Smiles. *San Diego Union-Tribune,* July 27, 1997.

Castro, Ed. "Jumping for Joy." *Desert Sun,* February 8, 1997.

Clark, Cheryl. "For these Ladies, 'Hoops' Are Not a Kind of Skirt." *San Diego Union-Tribune,* May 14, 1995.

Cowherd, Kevin. "Rock of Ages." *Los Angeles Times,* November 10, 1997.

Courtney, Will. "Burnside's a Grand Bodysurfer." *North County Times,* August 17, 1997.

Crump, Terrence. "Accentuating the Positive Has Kept Rev. Paul Klose Young." *New Hampshire Citizen,* November 21, 1994.

Dibsie, Patricia. "And So 71 Years Later, They Married." *San Diego Union-Tribune,* November 29, 1997.

Donnelly, Kathleen. "Fittingly, LaLanne Makes You Sit Up and Take Notice." *San Diego Union-Tribune,* August 31, 1995.

Farmer, Kevin." 'Golden Geezers' Still Out Taming the Waves." *North County Times,* August 18, 1996.

Fernane, Wendy. "Bowling for Independence." *Blade-Citizen,* October 4, 1995.

Fitzsimmons, Barbara. "Male Bonding." *San Diego Union-Tribune,* October 7, 1997.

Folmar, Kate. "'Legend' Taught Generations, and at 80, Is Still Ready to Ride." *Los Angeles Times,* July 20, 1997.

315

Grannan, Caroline. "Home Alone." *Los Angeles Times*, August 17, 1997.

Hansen, Leonard J. "Return to Fitness Produces Mature Adult Champions. *San Diego Union-Tribune,* July 26, 1995.

Herndon, Lucia. "Acting Very Much Like Family." *Philadelphia Inquirer,* March 19, 1997.

Hoekstra, Dave. "Red-Hot Mr. Bongo Still Scorches Skins." *Chicago Sun Times,* June 9, 1995.

Ireland, Philip K. "Vista Program Pairs Seniors, Students." *North County Times,* August 10, 1997.

Jaret, Peter. "Fitness and Age." *Vogue*, (February 1994).

Kay, Karen. "Sunbonnet Sue and Her Fountain of Youth." *Psychology for Living,* May 1989.

Kirkpatrick, Cliff. "Seniors Take New Friendship to 'Golden' Heights." *North County Times,* August 14, 1997.

Knox, Richard A. "People Living Longer in Era of Healthy Aging." *San Diego Union-Tribune,* April 8, 1998.

LaRue, Steve. "Legally Blind Seniors Ready for 12,000-mile Travel Adventure." *San Diego Union-Tribune,* January 3, 1995.

Levine, Bettijane. "Ageless Love." *Los Angeles Times*, August 13, 1997.

———. "The Sky's the Limit." *Los Angeles Times*, February 5, 1998.

Lyons, Christine. "Tellin' Tales." *AARP Bulletin* (September 1997).

Mascari-Bott, Paula. "A Grand Game for Grandma." *San Diego Union-Tribune,* July 12, 1997.

Matalon, Jean-Marc. Long, "Full Life Comes to an End." *San Diego Union-Tribune,* August 5, 1997.

McCarthy, Dennis. "Octogenerian Duo Teach Benefits of Exercise." *Daily News,* August 12, 1997.

Moehringer, J. R." 4 Cyclists Race to Slow Down Cycle of Life." *Los Angeles Times,* July 30, 1995.

Neleson, Denise. "Senior Is Head Over-Heels for Fitness." *San Diego Union-Tribune,* April 12, 1997.

Neville, Sheri C. "Riders Say Their Motorcycles Reflect their Lifestyle Choice." *Senior World,* April 1997.

Norcross, Don. "Old Reliable." *The San Diego Union-Tribune,* April 5, 1997.

———. "At 77, He's Teaching Kids New Tricks." *San Diego Union-Tribune,* October 29, 1996.

O'Connor, Colleen. "Over-62 Set Gets Its Kicks in Karate Class." *San Diego Union Tribune,* October 31, 1995.

Oliver, Myrna. "Hulda Crooks, 101; Oldest Woman to Scale Mt. Whitney." *Los Angeles Times,* November 26, 1997.

Ondash, E'louise. "The Changing Face of Sports." *North County Times,* October 13, 1997.

O'Sullivan, Carol. "Redefining Aging." *Delicious!* (May 1997).

Peters, Keith. "Jordan: Forever Young." *Palo Alto Weekly,* August 13, 1997.

Quintanilla, Michael. "The Human Tornado." *Los Angeles Times,* April 9, 1995.

Roan, Shari. "'Mother' Jones." *Los Angeles Times,* May 25, 1997.

Roberts, Ozzie. "Making It." *San Diego Union-Tribune,* April 17, 1997.

Rubin, Neal. "There's Nothing Vain about Having a Fashionable Cane. *San Diego Union-Tribune,* July 7, 1997.

Ryan, Michael. "He Has an Answer for Those Who Ask: Why?" *Parade Magazine,* September 21, 1997.

Sherman, Lola. "'Nun on the Run' Triumphs over Torture, Cancer." *San Diego Tribune,* April 6, 1989.

Sherman, Lola. "Woodcarver Still Going Strong—Months Shy of Notching 99. *San Diego Union-Tribune,* August 14, 1997.

Slaughter, Pamela. "Bridging the Gap." *The Blade-Citizen,* July 26, 1995.

Spitz, Katherine. "82-year-old Jack LaLanne Still Fired Up by Fitness Mission." *Daily News,* May 6, 1997.

Stewart, Jocelyn Y. "Age of Discovery." *Los Angeles Times,* June 20, 1997.

Tanner, Lindsey. "Runner Continues to Go the Distance, and Then Some." *North County Times,* August 4, 1996.

Tymn, Mike. "Man on the Run." *Honolulu Advertiser,* December 6, 1997.

Vose, Mary. "Seniors Pick Up the Pace." *Daily News,* June 4, 1996.

Weaver, Greg Lynn. "In the Footsteps of the Buddah." *Holistic Health Journal,* Autumn 1997.

Williams, Jack. "Relaxation the Taoist Way: Flowing Qi Gong." *San Diego Union-Tribune,* February 2, 1997.

Williams, Frank B. "Runners' Course." *Los Angeles Times,* February 26, 1995.

Kelly Ferrin has more than fifteen years of experience as a specialist in geron- tology. She is an active speaker, consultant and writer on a variety of aging issues. Kelly was one of the first to graduate from the University of Southern California's acclaimed Leonard Davis School of Gerontology. She is a certified AARP retirement specialist and serves as a con- sultant to the Governor's Council on Physical Fitness and Sports for older adults. Kelly lives with her husband in Carlsbad, California.

From Grandma With Love: A Legacy of Values
by Toni Thomas

Drawing upon the collective wisdom and experience of grandmothers across the country, these real-life experiences will warm your heart, remind you of your life, and inspire your young people to live character based lives. You will love these stories.

Your purchase will help needy children because 30% of all sales will be donated by ALTI Publishing to a joint program of the National Head Start Association, National Association of Foster Grandparent Program Directors, and the National Association of Retired and Senior Volunteer Program Directors.

This beautiful, illustrated, hardcover book won The Family Channel Seal of Quality and was a Literary Guild Book Club selection.

Hardcover, 160 pgs., 10" x 7", illustrations, $18.00. ISBN 1-883051-13-4

Volunteering: 101 Ways You Can Improve the World and Your Life
By Douglas M. Lawson, Ph.D.

Discover the joy of volunteering and how to get more from your service. A delightful guide answering all your questions. Ideal for both existing volunteers and beginners wanting to learn. Special sections for seniors.

Paperback, 144 pgs., 5 $1/2$" x 8 $1/2$", $7.95. ISBN 1-883051-17-7

As Good As I Want To Be:
A Parent's Guide to Help Your Teen Succeed
by Jack R. Christianson
Foreword by Steve Young, MVP Quarterback of the San Francisco 49ers.

What parent or grandparent doesn't want to help a young person succeed? This book is for:

- Parents who want more cooperation and love at home
- Parents/grandparents of problem children
- Those who want to accelerate their child's progress
- Teachers and youth leaders

You will enjoy the author's easy style and stories—and so will your child or grandchild. Tips for adults and young people.

Paperback, 208 pgs., 6" x 9", $12.95. ISBN 1-883051-19-3

Title	Price	# of Copies	Total $
What's Age Got To Do With It?	$14.95		
From Grandma With Love	$18.00		
As Good As I Want To Be	$12.95		
Volunteering: 101 Ways You Can Improve the World & Your Life	$ 7.95		
More Give To Live, (paperback)	$16.95		
More Give To Live, (hardcover)	$24.00		
"The Message" (video)	$8.95		
Subtotal			
Tax (California residents add 7.75%)			
Shipping & handling ($3.50 for 1 copy plus $.75 for each additional item)			
TOTAL			

Payment accepted by check, money order or credit card. Make checks-

payable to ALTI Publishing.

Name _____ Phone # _____

Address _____

City _____ State _____ Zip _____

VISA ☐ MC ☐ AMEX ☐

Card Number _____ Exp.Date _____

Signature _____

ALTI Publishing, 15708 Pomerado Rd, Ste. 209, Poway, CA 92064

(QUANTITY DISCOUNTS AVAILABLE)